Class and Social Mobility

ISSUES

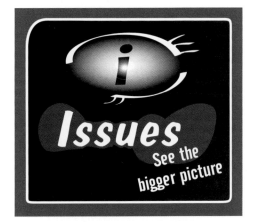

Volume 219

Series Editor

Lisa Firth

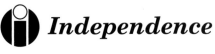

Independence

Educational Publishers

Cambridge

First published by Independence

The Studio, High Green

Great Shelford

Cambridge CB22 5EG

England

© Independence 2012

Copyright

This book is sold subject to the condition that it shall not,
by way of trade or otherwise, be lent, resold, hired out or otherwise
circulated in any form of binding or cover other than that in which it
is published without the publisher's prior consent.

Photocopy licence

The material in this book is protected by copyright. However, the
purchaser is free to make multiple copies of particular articles for instructional
purposes for immediate use within the purchasing institution.
Making copies of the entire book is not permitted.

British Library Cataloguing in Publication Data

Class and social mobility. -- (Issues ; v. 219)

1. Class consciousness--Great Britain. 2. Social classes--

Great Britain. 3. Great Britain--Social conditions--21st

century.

I. Series II. Firth, Lisa.

305.5-dc23

ISBN-13: 978 1 86168 604 6

Printed in Great Britain

MWL Print Group Ltd

CONTENTS

Chapter 1 Class and Inequality

Chapter 2 Social Mobility

A note on critical evaluation

Because the information reprinted here is from a number of different sources, readers should bear in mind the origin of the text and whether the source is likely to have a particular bias when presenting information (just as they would if undertaking their own research). It is hoped that, as you read about the many aspects of the issues explored in this book, you will critically evaluate the information presented. It is important that you decide whether you are being presented with facts or opinions. Does the writer give a biased or an unbiased report? If an opinion is being expressed, do you agree with the writer?

Class and Social Mobility offers a useful starting point for those who need convenient access to information about the many issues involved. However, it is only a starting point. Following each article is a URL to the relevant organisation's website, which you may wish to visit for further information.

Uncovered: the real Middle Britain

Experian identifies Slough as social heartland of Middle Britain today.

If you live in a semi-detached house in Slough, drive a Ford Focus, shop at Tesco and can't find enough hours in your day, you could well have joined the ranks of the UK's biggest social group: Middle Britain.

Framed against the perennial debate about who or what constitutes Middle Britain, and increasing use of the term Middle Britain as a societal reference point, Experian has today painted a revealing new picture of the most talked about demographic in Britain today. Based on insight using Mosaic, Experian's consumer classification tool, this fresh perspective challenges typical notions about Middle Britain and looks beyond average income and class stereotypes to encompass characteristics, attitudes, behaviours and locations.

Experian has defined Middle Britain using Mosaic, which uses over 400 social and economic variables to better understand consumers. In Experian's view, Middle Britain today is represented by 13.1 million people making up nearly a quarter of the population (21%). This definition of Middle Britain is based on a series of key statistical measures including income, age, car ownership, type of house, number of holidays, attitudes and behaviours. Based on Experian's analysis, the picture that emerges of Middle Britain is of a group that is pressurised, faces many challenges and is more complex than might be expected. Middle Britain is no longer epitomised just by middle managers living with their families in leafy suburbs but instead spans the full cultural spectrum of UK life – taking in both single-person households and married couples of all ages living in brownfield inner city locations, through to the outer edges of large towns and cities as well as affluent suburbs.

According to Experian's analysis, the place in the UK with the highest density of people personifying Middle Britain today is Slough, with almost two-thirds of the population here (63%) falling into the Middle Britain band.

In fact, Experian's analysis suggests that Middle Britain represents almost a quarter of the UK population (21%). Interestingly, Hindus and Sikhs are 1.6 times and 1.8 times more likely to be in Middle Britain compared to the UK average.

Nigel Wilson, Managing Director of Experian Marketing Information Services, UK and Ireland, said: 'Middle Britain is often discussed yet it has rarely been examined in a meaningful way, taking into account behaviours and consumer habits. We need to dispel the myth that Middle Britain is simply either those on average incomes or is somehow synonymous with being middle class – it takes in a much broader sweep of the population than either of those two descriptors. It's essentially a new consumer order.

'Slough is a microcosm of Middle Britain today – a melting pot of classes and cultures. It forms a corner of a Middle Britain triangle shared with Harrow in the north and Bexley in the south-east that absolutely encapsulates why more of us are members of Middle Britain than we might think.'

Middle Britain traits

Middle Britain in 2010 comes in two flavours – those living in older, more established suburbs such as Bexley or Harrow and areas of more modern housing and a younger population such as Thurrock, Slough or Milton Keynes. Middle Britain today is 2.5 times more likely than the national average to live in a semi-detached house and 14% of this group live in new properties – compared to a UK average of only 6%.

Based on Experian's Mosaic analysis, Middle Britons in the older suburbs are increasingly worried about rising fees and costs, having difficulty in covering their mortgage and at the same time facing reduced pension values. Coupled with this, parents in this group are also concerned about the challenges their children are tackling: for example, university debt and getting on the housing ladder. Middle Britain's other side is younger and lives in predominantly newer housing. In places around Eastleigh and Dartford the younger Middle Briton worries about high mortgages, job security and high levels of debts.

Despite these differences between the mature enclaves of Middle Britain and its new neighbours, inhabitants have a common set of characteristics. Experian's research shows that whilst 54% of Middle Britain are

EXPERIAN

happy with their standard of living, 60% acknowledge that 'in this day and age it is important to juggle various tasks at the same time'. Middle Britain today struggles with finding enough hours in the day (57%) yet displays optimism in admitting they can change their life if they want to.

Home is where the heart is

Family is very important to Middle Britons: many have children, which is a major influence on their leisure time. This group tends to have a low-key social life, encompassing the gym and local cinema, trips to the seaside, parks and theme parks. They also choose to spend much of their leisure time at home. Not only are days out planned with the kids in mind, but even at home, this group is more likely than the rest of the UK to watch children's programmes, with sci-fi/fantasy and property genres also popular.

Conscious of their health, many are members of the gym, running is popular amongst parents of primary school children and cycling is a regular pastime amongst families with children of all ages. Martial arts are a stand-out pastime of younger Middle Britain. When it comes to watching sport, football, as with the rest of the UK, is the overall favourite (30%) although Middle Britons are more likely to watch extreme sports (e.g. skateboarding) compared to the rest of the UK.

Middle Britain in the digital age

Experian's data shows that Middle Britons are huge technology consumers and by 2015 their spending on communications technology will increase by over 40%.

Many are parents juggling busy working lives, making them frequent Internet bankers and shoppers. As experienced users of technology at work, they take a strong interest in the latest digital gizmos and gadgets. In the newer neighbourhoods, Middle Britain's consumers rely on searching the Internet for information and advice about products and services, with 50% using the Internet as their preferred channel for making purchases.

This group's favoured means of communicating socially is through using the Internet (31%), more than the telephone (29%) and email (23%). It perhaps comes as no surprise, then, that Facebook is the second most visited website by this group, after Google. However, if mobile and Internet providers are going to benefit, it is the hospitality industry that stands to lose out on the Middle Britain pound with a spending on bars, hotels and restaurants set to decrease by 3% by 2015 according to Experian's economists.

Middle Britain's spending power?

Household income for Middle Britain is around 10% higher than the national average at £47,300 per year. Although outgoings are also higher, mainly in terms of income

tax and mortgage commitments, disposable income is nonetheless 8% higher than the national average. Almost half (48%) of Middle Britons perceive themselves 'coping financially' rather than being 'financially comfortable' (29%).

By 2015, Experian's economists forecast that Middle Britain's average income is expected to grow by about 6.6% in real terms – slightly higher than the national average of 6%. However, outgoings are likely to increase faster than the national average with the net result that Middle Britain's disposable income is set to increase by 2.7% by 2015. However, this group is likely to be more exposed than the general population to increases in mortgage interest rates over the coming years.

Brands are important to this group and buying decisions are governed by both value for money and technical excellence. Experian's research shows that whilst almost half (44%) state that they plan their weekly shopping carefully, almost a third (31%) also admit to buying the cheapest product. Word-of-mouth endorsement holds particular sway and this group is increasingly open to text-based marketing over direct mail.

Nigel Wilson continued: 'Middle Britain has to become a consumer touchstone for companies. This is a group that represents a broad section of society and has the power to make or break a brand. Unlike the traditional stereotypes, our analysis shows that Middle Britain encompasses a variety of ages, ethnic backgrounds, likes and dislikes, as well as being scattered across the country. With our research showing how technology-savvy this group is, successful brands will be the ones that tap into what these consumers really want from the companies they deal with by using personalised, relevant and timely digital content.'
14 December 2010

⇨ The above information is reprinted with kind permission from Experian. Visit www.experian.co.uk for more.

© Experian

Local Authority	Ranking	% of population falling under Middle Britain
Slough	1	62.59%
Rushmoor	2	56.01%
Bexley	3	53.02%
Spelthorne	4	51.43%
Harrow	5	49.70%
Bracknell Forest	6	49.28%
Broxbourne	7	49.00%
Hillingdon	8	48.90%
Dartford	9	47.13%
Milton Keynes	10	47.06%

Source: Experian

EXPERIAN

Celebrate your identity!
That is, know your place

A new report says fewer workers now define themselves as 'working class'. Maybe they're rebelling against the stifling politics of identity.

By Brendan O'Neill

> In a speech in London last night, spiked editor Brendan O'Neill debated Owen Jones, author of *Chavs: The Demonisation of the Working Classes*, on who or what is giving the lower orders a rough time today. O'Neill's opening comments are published below.

If you ever watch the later films of Mike Leigh, you will notice that all of them have a recurring character. From *High Hopes* through to *Secrets & Lies* through to *Vera Drake*, this character always, always makes an appearance.

And the character is that person who has left his or her working-class community. That person who has turned their back on their working-class roots and foolishly gone off in pursuit of the middle-class dream.

The character is usually a woman. She is always miserable and soulless. She lives in a big but heartless house, full of perfectly polished ornaments. And she is forever committing embarrassing social *faux pas*, which of course middle-class Mike Leigh fans find hilarious. Leaving aside *Topsy Turvy*, I challenge you to find any recent Mike Leigh film which doesn't feature that character.

And it's a character which speaks to a very powerful prejudice amongst today's liberal elite – a prejudice which says that there is something weird, something unnatural, something morally dubious about working-class people who leave their communities.

It is seen as an act of betrayal. They have abandoned community solidarity and have been won over by, or rather have been brainwashed by, the rampant Thatcherite culture of consumption and one-upmanship.

In answer to the question of who or what is demonising the working classes today, I would say that that prejudice is one of the most decisive things. That prejudice against working-class people with ambition, against working-class people who aspire to own more stuff or to move to nicer, leafier suburbs or simply to have The Good Life, is really the driving force behind modern liberal snobbery.

It's a prejudice which has been around for nearly 30 years. Right from Loadsamoney through to the attacks on 'Essex Man' and 'Basildon Man' through to the assaults on yuppies, with their vulgar fast cars and their vulgar common accents – working-class people with material aspirations have had a special place in the middle-class canon of hate figures.

They are often depicted as fishes out of water, trying to live a life that they are hilariously ill-suited for. So one group that everyone loves to mock is the footballer's wife, drinking her Chardonnay, living in a ghastly Mock Tudor mansion, ruining Tuscany for everyone else by insisting on holidaying there. Who do these people think they are? What are they doing in our social circles?

That sentiment was explicitly expressed in a *Guardian* article about a nouveau-riche nightclub frequented by the footballer Wayne Rooney. It described the club as 'a tawdry place where the clientele seem to be under the misapprehension that drinking champagne is a symbol of class'.

And it is that prejudice against the grasping, greedy sections of the lower orders which fuelled the attack on so-called chavs in recent years. Chavs are mocked for having bling, for their love of fashion labels, for daring to wear Burberry, which of course only posh people can really carry off.

Ironically, the so-called defenders of 'chavs' also buy into this prejudice. So in his book, Mr Jones favourably quotes Hazel Blears as saying: 'I've never understood the term "social mobility" because that implies you want to get out of somewhere… And I think there is a great deal to be said for making who you are something to be proud of.' In other words, know your place. The one thing that chav-bashers and chav-defenders share in common is a profound discomfort with working-class individual aspiration.

This liberal prejudice has even been given the stamp of scientific authority in recent years. Books by the psychologist Oliver James and the social scientist Richard Wilkinson claim it is a provable fact that our desire for more and more stuff makes us mentally ill. If you chase after material goods you will catch a disease known as 'Affluenza'. That is how powerful and deeply ingrained the liberal disgust for aspirant working-class people has become: it has been turned into 'science'.

What is behind this relentless cultural demonisation of working-class people who might want to leave their

communities or create new lives for themselves? I think there are two points to make about this prejudice.

Firstly, it is just wrong. It is wrong to make such a savage distinction between good working-class people who stay in their communities and bad working-class people who abandon them. Or between 'rugged individualism', which is seen as bad, and 'community spirit', which is seen as good. In fact those two things inform and reinforce each other.

There is far more interplay between the individual and the community than this childish prejudice lets on. Often the youthful ambitions of working-class individuals will actually be nurtured by their family and friends, who want them to go somewhere better. And those individuals who do leave and who do make loadsamoney almost always keep a connection with their community: they might employ their old working-class friends or they might send a weekly cheque to their mother or grandmother.

The idea that it is bad to be socially mobile, and by extension that it is good to be socially immobile, is really just a rehabilitation of the old sneering prejudice that the poor should not get ideas above their station.

And the second point about this prejudice, which is far more powerful on the left than it is on the right, is that it speaks to a profound shift that has taken place in left-wing thinking in recent years. It speaks to a shift from focusing on 'class consciousness' to focusing on 'class identity'; from treating working class as a political and social condition to treating it as a permanent and fixed identity.

In the past, radical left-wing thinkers, even some champagne socialists, were more interested in 'class consciousness'. They were more interested in the working class becoming conscious of its position as a class and of its power to overthrow the class system. Indeed, the aim of radical left-wing activism was really to bring about the end of the working class.

Today, liberal and left-wing thinkers are obsessed with 'class identity'. They have turned being working class from a social predicament, a social status, into a fixed cultural identity. They see it, not as something that might be and maybe even should be brought to an end, but as something that should be celebrated.

So they go all misty-eyed for the culture and values and spirit of these noble savages, and at the same time they have created a whole armoury of abuse and insults for any working-class person who dares to reject his identity and to try to become something else. In their fatalistic, identity-obsessed outlook, the working-class person who leaves his community is not simply trying to 'get on' – he is sinning against the natural order of things, against his fixed position in the world, against the whole politics of identity. Their embrace of the idea that working class is an identity, rather than a product of the capitalist system, makes them furiously hostile to anybody who dares to break out of that. Ironically, in such circumstances, the man or woman who rebels against his working-class identity, as defined for him or her by others, is striking a far better blow for working-class self-respect and self-determination than those middle-class outsiders who say: 'Be proud of who you are.'

It's no wonder, then, that according to a report published by the think-tank Britain Thinks last week, fewer and fewer workers are describing themselves as 'working class'. When being 'working class' no longer means being powerful and transformative, but instead means knowing your place and living like a permanent exhibit in a cultural zoo that will apparently exist forever, it isn't surprising that people want to wriggle free from that. Maybe they are refusing to accept the Fate designed for them by those middle-class celebrators of the old, decent, back-broken working class. And of course when they refuse to accept that fate, by making loadsamoney or by draping themselves in bling, they are severely chastised for their disobedience.

In truth, there is nothing permanent about being working class. The working class has only existed for a few hundred years, and there is no reason that this class should still exist in a few hundred years from now. I hope it doesn't. And I hope that the next working-class uprising will be against the elitist and middle-class do-gooders who encourage working people to revel in their identity, as if they are going to live like this and work like this forever.

6 July 2011

⇨ Information from Spiked Online. Visit www.spiked-online.com for more.

© *Spiked Online*

CLIMBING THE ASPIRATIONAL LADDER

Traitor!

SPIKED

Chav: the vile word at the heart of fractured Britain

Fostering the loathing of a feral underclass allows public resentment to be diverted from those above to those below.

By Polly Toynbee

That word slips out. This time it was used by a Lib Dem peer on the Equality and Human Rights Commission. Baroness Hussein-Ece tweeted: 'Help. Trapped in a queue in chav land. Woman behind me explaining latest EastEnders plot to mate while eating largest bun I've ever seen.' When challenged, she said she hadn't meant chav in any derogatory way. Of course not. But take a look at the venomous class-hate site ChavTowns to see what lies beneath.

She would presumably never say [racially abusive terms such as] n****r or P**i, but chav is acceptable class abuse by people asserting superiority over those they despise. Poisonous class bile is so ordinary that our future king and his brother played at dressing up and talking funny at a chav party mocking their lower-class subjects.

Wrapped inside this little word is the quintessence of Britain's great social fracture. Over the last 30 years the public monstering of a huge slice of the population by luckier, better-paid people has become commonplace. This is language from the Edwardian era of unbridled snobbery. When safely reproduced in *Downton Abbey*, as the lady sneering at the scullery maid or the landowner bullying his workers, we are encouraged to look back smugly as if these shocking class differences were long gone. The form and style may have changed – but the reality of extreme inequality and self-confident class contempt is back.

> *Public perception of the shape of society has been so warped that most no longer know how others live, where they stand in relation to the rest, who earns what or why*

That brief period between 1917 and 1979, when British wealth, trembling in fear of revolution, ceded some power, opportunity and money to the working classes is over. There are now no politics to express or admit the enormity of what has happened since the 1980s – how wealth and human respect drained from the bottom to enrich and glorify the top.

Public perception of the shape of society has been so warped that most no longer know how others live, where they stand in relation to the rest, who earns what or why. By deliberate misrepresentation, drip, drip, week after week, the powerful interests of wealth deliberately distort reality. The best weapon in the class armoury fosters loathing of a 'feral underclass' – its size vague and never delineated, relying on anecdotes of extreme dysfunction, of which any society has plenty. One sneer cleverly elides millions of low-earning workers in equal chav contempt for all living on an estate, drawing any benefit – even if in work – as cheats, addicts and layabouts. That's the way to divert resentment from those above, to those below.

Here's a prime example. On this quiet bank holiday weekend, Iain Duncan Smith's department deposited a dirty little non-story on the doormat of his favourite newspapers. Headlined 'No More Excuses', the press release lists 'the ten top worst excuses used by benefit cheats'. They include 'I wasn't using the ladder to clean windows, I carried it for my bad back', and 'It wasn't me working, it was my identical twin'.

Less than one person in four now defines as working class.

Class	Percentage
Upper	0%
Upper middle	7%
Middle	43%
Lower middle	21%
Working	24%
Not sure	4%

Source: What about the workers?, Britainthinks, June 2011.

THE GUARDIAN

There are no figures to say how many people put up the sort of ludicrous pleas heard daily in any magistrate court. Department for Work and Pensions figures are anyway wobbly. Last year David Cameron declared war on benefit fraudsters, calling in special agents to deal with £5.2bn fraud and error in the benefits bill – worth, he said, 200 secondary schools and 150,000 nurses. Cathy Newman's excellent Channel 4 FactCheck found £1.5bn of that was fraud and the rest error.

This latest DWP press release says fraud is now £1.6bn. That's a walloping sum – but let's put it in proportion. It's still only 0.7% of the benefits bill. Many a company would be proud of such a low loss from theft. The attorney general's National Fraud Authority found £38.4bn lost to fraud last year. Most fraud is in the finance industry – £3.6bn – though it's only 9% of the economy. That's more than is stolen in retail – a larger sector. Meanwhile, £15bn was officially caught in tax fraud, while estimated tax avoidance is £70bn.

But never mind, benefit stories are eye-catching and they do the job intended: they make us mean and ungenerous, stifling protest at Duncan Smith's monumental £18bn benefits cut. Such tales spread a wider loathing of a whole perceived class, of anyone on benefits. With most of the poor in work, that includes battalions of the low-paid whose miserable pay is topped up by tax credits to stop them starving. But a few choice anecdotes are worth a ton of statistics. That ladder! Ha!

I am on the circulation list for all DWP press releases, so why didn't I get this one and why wasn't this tacky rubbish put up on their website? 'We only sent it out to a couple of our key contacts,' said the duty press officer yesterday – that was the *Mail* and the *Telegraph*. 'It was a soft consumer story, a PR story we sold proactively, so we didn't sell it any wider.' So that's how Iain Duncan Smith does it these days, 'selling' to friendly buyers only.

Anecdotes smearing all on housing benefit or tax credits help make the working class disappear. In his 1997 triumph, Tony Blair declared class over, we're all middle class – except for a 'socially excluded' lumpen rump. 'The new Britain is a meritocracy,' he declared – not as a future goal but as a fact. So who are the eight million in manual jobs and the eight million clerks and sales assistants who make up half the workforce?

In my book *Hard Work*, I reported on the remarkably strong work ethic of those in jobs paying little more than benefits, the carers and cleaners doing essential work well, despite lack of money or respect. In *Unjust Rewards*, David Walker and I charted how since the decline of the unions people have lost their bearings on class and incomes: the mega-wealthy are clueless about ordinary earnings and even the poor are misled into thinking their pay is quite middling.

Aspiration and social mobility are the useful mirage, laying blame squarely with individuals who should try harder to escape their families and friends, instead of seeking great fairness for all. It suits life's winners to pretend this is a meritocracy: we well-off deserve our luck, anyone can join us if they try.

A superb and angry new book, *Chavs* by Owen Jones, published next week, pulls together the welter of evidence on the demonisation of the working class. Read it for a strong analysis of the conspiracy to deny the very existence of a working class, even to itself. New Labour colluded with this vanishing act but Ed Miliband's espousal of the 'squeezed middle' may be tiptoeing towards giving a voice back to the great disappeared.

31 May 2011

© Guardian News and Media Limited 2011

THE GUARDIAN

The 50p tax rate must go – but scrapping it could provoke an all-out class war

By Daniel Knowles

Boris Johnson's column this morning is a classic – a defence of the entrepreneurial and lively (or tennis players at least) combined with a mild attack on the Treasury. Boris wants the 50p rate to go, pointing out that ridiculously, even the French now have a lower highest rate than us. This extreme burden deters not just sportsmen, but also entrepreneurs, investors and top-flight professionals, perhaps even costing us tax revenue in the process.

On the economics, Boris is undoubtedly right. For a year or two, hiking up taxes to raise revenue works: it's not worth the trouble of moving to Switzerland if you only dodge one year's tax. But over time, the peak of what economists call the Laffer curve shifts – progressively, you raise less money as people react to higher taxes. Eventually, you reach a point where you're actually losing revenue. So the case for outlining a firm timetable to scrap the 50p rate is a strong one. That is why George Osborne has hinted that the tax won't last beyond 2013.

A poll for The Times in 2009 found that 57 per cent of people are in favour of keeping the higher rate, while just 22 per cent oppose it

But while the economic case is strong, the politics is less easy. A poll for *The Times* in 2009 found that 57 per cent of people are in favour of keeping the higher rate, while just 22 per cent oppose it. Those numbers will probably shift as the destructiveness of the policy becomes clearer, but when real living standards are being squeezed by other tax rises – VAT and National Insurance in particular – it won't be easy to argue for a tax cut that mostly benefits bankers.

Unfortunately, while Tony Blair or Margaret Thatcher could sell the idea of an entrepreneurial culture, George Gideon Oliver Osborne, heir to the Osborne baronetcy, is more likely to just look self-interested. According to YouGov, fully 79 per cent of people think that the Conservatives represent 'the rich'. Though it may be unfair, the charge that Tories are cutting taxes for their friends will always stick – especially to George Osborne, a Tory especially likely to inspire outrageous class hatred.

Anticipating this, the Chancellor will want to prepare the ground carefully – he needs to remind the public of the need for competitiveness, not just austerity. Osborne might also be helped by Labour's indecision – Ed Miliband has hinted he might want to make the tax permanent, but others in the Labour party are less keen. By 2013, if the economy has recovered enough, it might be possible to treat the 50p rate as a redundant emergency measure, either with Labour's support, or by capitalising on the party's splits.

But it is equally likely that the economy won't much recover, while the squeeze on middle-class incomes will carry on. Labour might even unify against a tax cut. What does George Osborne do then? One thing seems certain: the conundrum would help Boris Johnson's leadership campaign no end.

4 July 2011

© Telegraph Media Group Limited 2011

THE TELEGRAPH

Inherited wealth and inequality

Information from the ToUChstone blog.

By Richard Exell

Inherited wealth makes the UK an even more unequal country than some of us had realised. Most of the time, egalitarians like me tend to concentrate our worrying on unequal incomes, but every so often something new reminds us about other forms of inequality.

One of these prompts is *Recent trends in the size and the distribution of inherited wealth in the UK*, a new study by Eleni Karagiannaki from the Centre for the Analysis of Social Exclusion at the London School of Economics, which shows that on a common measure of inequality, inherited wealth is two or three times as unequal as incomes.

'Any increase in the Inheritance Tax threshold would represent a reallocation of wealth to the very wealthy'

This study of inherited wealth from 1984 to 2005 found that rising house prices pushed up the value of inheritances from being worth 3% of GDP in 1984 to about 4.3% in 2005 and there is a 'high degree of inequality' in the distribution of inheritances.

A common measure of inequality is the Gini coefficient – a society with perfect equality would have a Gini coefficient of 0.00, one where one person had all the wealth would score 1.00. Depending on the survey used for the data and the measure of inheritance, the study found that the Gini coefficient for inherited wealth ranged from 0.90 to 0.97.

That is the figure when we include all respondents: if the results are limited to people who had had some inheritance, the range is 0.62 to 0.75.

For comparison, the Gini coefficient for income inequality in 2009/10 was 0.36 for income before housing costs and 0.40 after housing costs. And those of us who complain about inequality worry a great deal about these figures.

The study concludes with an interesting policy discussion. Inheritance Tax is not charged on estates below £325,000 and married couples and civil partners can effectively double this up to £650,000. Given the inequality of inherited wealth, this means that Inheritance Tax is only paid by 'a minority of very wealthy estates' and: 'Any increase in the Inheritance Tax threshold would represent a reallocation of wealth to the very wealthy.'

20 July 2011

⇨ The above information is reprinted with kind permission from the ToUChstone blog. Visit http://touchstoneblog.org.uk for more information on this and other related topics.

© ToUChstone blog

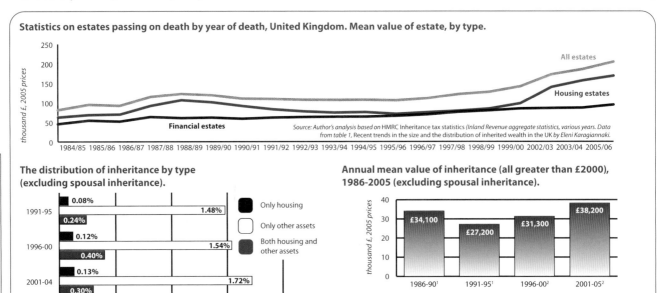

Statistics on estates passing on death by year of death, United Kingdom. Mean value of estate, by type.

All estates

Housing estates

Financial estates

thousand £, 2005 prices

1984/85 1985/86 1986/87 1987/88 1988/89 1989/90 1990/91 1991/92 1992/93 1993/94 1994/95 1995/96 1996/97 1997/98 1998/99 1999/00 2002/03 2003/04 2005/06

Source: Author's analysis based on HMRC Inheritance tax statistics (Inland Revenue aggregate statistics, various years. Data from table 1, Recent trends in the size and the distribution of inherited wealth in the UK by Eleni Karagiannaki).

The distribution of inheritance by type (excluding spousal inheritance).

1991-95: 0.08%, 1.48%, 0.24%
1996-00: 0.12%, 1.54%, 0.40%
2001-04: 0.13%, 1.72%, 0.30%

■ Only housing
□ Only other assets
▨ Both housing and other assets

% 0.0   0.5   1.0   1.5   2.0

Source: Author's analysis using the Attitudes to Inheritance survey. Data from table 4, Recent trends in the size and the distribution of inherited wealth in the UK by Eleni Karagiannaki.

Annual mean value of inheritance (all greater than £2000), 1986-2005 (excluding spousal inheritance).

thousand £, 2005 prices

1986-90[1]: £34,100
1991-95[1]: £27,200
1996-00[2]: £31,300
2001-05[2]: £38,200

1. Figures from the General Household Survey.
2. Figures from the British Household Panel Survey.

Source: Author's analysis using the 1995/96 General Household Survey and the British Household Panel Survey (waves 7-16). Data from table 3, Recent trends in the size and the distribution of inherited wealth in the UK by Eleni Karagiannaki.

TOUCHSTONE BLOG

Seven in ten of us belong to Middle Britain

A major new survey into social attitudes identifies six tribes among the nation's aspirational classes. John Rentoul and Matt Chorley examine the report's fascinating and provocative findings.

An unprecedented shift in public attitudes heralding a huge rise in the nation's middle classes is revealed today by the most comprehensive study of British society ever conducted. The report shows a huge rise in the country's aspirations, with seven in ten Britons now viewing themselves as middle class, compared with a quarter a generation ago.

The survey, carried out by the new research company BritainThinks and published exclusively by *The Independent on Sunday*, also discloses that only 24 per cent of people now describe themselves as working class – and no one labels him or herself upper class any more.

This explosion in the size of Middle Britain – with six distinct tribes of the middle class identified through detailed focus group and statistical analysis – has profound implications for economic and public policy and for how politicians frame their pitch to the electorate, particularly to the three groups of swing voters who decide elections.

So vast is the cohort now describing itself as middle class that it ranges from cafétière-pouring, *Telegraph*-reading retirees, more prone to voting Conservative and with annual household income of almost £47,000,

to the aspirant soap addicts struggling to make ends meet on less than £30,000. The average working-class household income is £24,000.

But while the vast majority of the nation sees itself as middle class, it seems that aspirant lifestyles are in peril, with people's anxiety about jobs, housing and the environment leading to fears that their children's future will be bleaker than their own.

The comprehensive analysis, of everything from Marks & Spencer to *The X Factor*, reveals widely differing views about the realities of being middle class in Britain. BritainThinks conducted an opinion poll of 2,003 people, backed up by focus groups to probe attitudes in more depth. The research paints a picture of a large middle class, some parts of which fear that their recent rise will be reversed in hard economic times, but which is still mostly optimistic.

But while the vast majority of the nation sees itself as middle class, it seems that aspirant lifestyles are in peril

---

It shines a spotlight on the major political battleground of the next four years, with middle-class people most likely to vote. Ed Miliband, the Labour leader, is targeting what he calls the 'squeezed middle' that is feeling the pinch. Nick Clegg has characterised this group as Alarm Clock Britons – lower-paid workers who cannot afford private healthcare or education. So far, the Conservatives have struggled to persuade voters the Government is on their side. The survey found that David Cameron is regarded as the poshest of a list of 29 famous people.

People who define themselves as middle class are more likely than the working class to choose the words 'hopeful' and 'proud' to describe how they feel about their family's future. By contrast, the shrinking working class seems to feel beleaguered, and people who describe themselves as working class are more likely to choose words such as 'worried', 'fearful' and 'depressed' to describe how they feel.

Those who describe themselves as middle class have an average household income of £37,000 a year. Almost half of the middle class say that they have over £10,000 in savings, compared with one-fifth of the working class.

THE INDEPENDENT

But the new middle class encompasses wide differences of income, wealth and attitudes. BritainThinks researchers used the data to identify six segments of the middle class. Their average household incomes range from £29,500 a year among the 'Squeezed Strugglers' to £47,000 among the 'Deserving Downtimers', the richest group of mainly older people, most of whom have retired.

Political attitudes are sharply divergent too, with two groups solidly Conservative (the Deserving Downtimers and the *Daily Mail* Disciplinarians), one strongly Labour (the Stretched Strugglers) and the other three described as 'marginal'. These three groups – the Comfortable Greens, Urban Networkers and Bargain Hunters – make up the prime electoral battleground. Those who call themselves middle class are much more likely to vote (69 per cent) than the working class (55 per cent).

The survey paints the fullest picture yet of changing attitudes towards class in Britain today, to which *The Independent on Sunday* devotes this special issue. The most important factor defining a person's class is 'level of education', according to 23 per cent, followed by 'their parents' class' (21 per cent), 'the nature of their job' (20 per cent) and 'their income' (20 per cent).

One of the most striking differences is that 51 per cent of working-class respondents agree with 'I often have conversations with friends about shows like *The X Factor*', while only 29 per cent of the middle class do.

Deborah Mattinson, director of BritainThinks, asked middle-class participants in the focus groups to bring with them an object that they thought symbolised their class. The most popular was a cafétière, and other objects included a book about Mozart, theatre tickets, a Kindle e-reader, an expensive bottle of brandy, a box of speciality teas, a Cath Kidston bottle warmer and a ski hat. 'I'm just a snob maybe. I won't have instant coffee,' said one focus group member. Another said of a cafétière: 'I take it with me when I travel. I like good coffee.'

The opinion survey found that in a list of 29 well-known people, Mr Cameron was the only one whom more people described as upper class than middle class. The next poshest, Kate Middleton, is regarded as upper middle class, as are Mr Clegg and Mr Miliband. In one focus group Mr Miliband was called an Etonian, along with the Prime Minister. The most middle-class person on the list was Sir Trevor McDonald, the former newsreader.

The middle class, as defined by people's self-image, is much larger than that generated by the commonly-used designations: the ABC1 social groups, categorised by occupation, are a little over half of the population, with skilled manual workers, shop workers and unemployed people (C2DE) described as working class.

The 71 per cent figure for the self-defined middle class is the highest recorded in an opinion survey, and includes seven per cent who describe themselves as 'upper middle' class, 43 per cent 'middle' and 21 per cent 'lower middle'. Only 24 per cent of the sample described themselves as working class; four per cent were 'not sure', and no respondents described themselves as 'upper' class. In the 1980s, by contrast, 27 per cent described themselves as middle or upper middle class in annual British Social Attitudes surveys.

This shift is reflected in focus groups, according to Ms Mattinson. C1/C2 swing voters in the 1980s would 'shrink from placing themselves' in the middle class; they tended to say that they wanted to 'better themselves'. Now, she says, many of them have done precisely that and are happy to describe themselves as middle class.

BritainThinks commissioned Populus Data Services to survey 2,003 British adults online, 11-14 December 2010. The six middle-class segments were identified using multivariate analysis, and six focus groups recruited to be representative of each group.

For more about BritainThinks, visit britainthinks.com
20 March 2011

© The Independent

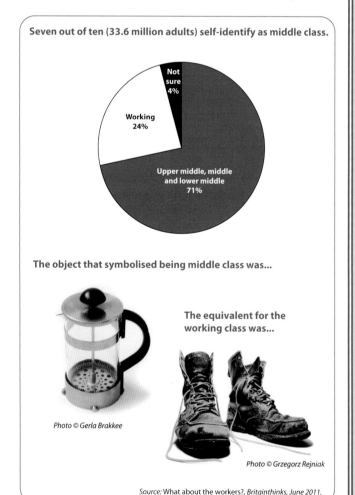

Seven out of ten (33.6 million adults) self-identify as middle class.

- Not sure 4%
- Working 24%
- Upper middle, middle and lower middle 71%

The object that symbolised being middle class was...

Photo © Gerla Brakkee

The equivalent for the working class was...

Photo © Grzegorz Rejniak

Source: What about the workers?, Britainthinks, June 2011.

Health and social class

Information from Patient UK.

By Dr Laurence Knott

Background

There has always been an association between health and social class and, despite the welfare state and the improvement in health in all sections of societies over the years, this discrepancy remains. It applies to all aspects of health, including expectation of life, infant and maternal mortality and general level of health. Whilst the failure to close the social gap is a disgrace to some, others would claim that so long as these parameters are improving in all levels of society there is no cause for concern. Despite 62 years of the National Health Service, there remain marked differences in all parameters of health across the social classes. Women continue to live longer than men but the gap is closing. Based on 2007-09 mortality rates, a man aged 65 could expect to live another 17.6 years and a woman aged 65 another 20.2 years.

Social class is a complex issue that may involve status, wealth, culture, background and employment. The relationship between class and ill health is not simple. There are a number of different influences on health, some of which include social class. This is demonstrated by multilevel analysis (a method of assessing health inequalities using several different factors) which shows health inequalities even between households living in the same street. In 1943, Sigerist, following the line of Virchow, wrote, 'The task of medicine is to promote health, to prevent disease, to treat the sick when prevention is broken down and to rehabilitate the people after they have been cured. These are highly social functions and we must look at medicine as basically a social science.'

The greatest influences on the improvement in health with longer expectancy of life, lower infant mortality, etc. have been not so much medical discoveries as improved social conditions. One study in America found that, despite improvements in cancer detection and treatment, disparities in cancer mortality rates are chiefly related to race and social class.

History

In 1572, an Elizabethan Act made provision for the punishment of sturdy beggars and the relief of the impotent poor. A similar law followed in Scotland in 1574. In England, an Act of 1601 made provision for 'setting the poor on work'. This did not generally include accommodation but, in 1631, a workhouse was established in Abingdon and, in 1697, the Bristol Workhouse was established by private Act of Parliament. Scotland had 'houses of correction' established in the burghs, by an Act of 1672. Some people regarded all this as too liberal and, in 1834, Malthus argued that the population was increasing beyond the ability of the country to feed it. The Poor Law was seen as an encouragement to illegitimacy and this would lead in turn to mass starvation.

Edwin Chadwick published his *General Report on the Sanitary Conditions of the Labouring Population of Great Britain* in 1842. This showed that the average age at death in Liverpool at that time was 35 for gentry and professionals but only 15 for labourers, mechanics and servants. In 1901, Seebohm Rowntree was able not only to trace in detail the sanitary defects of areas of York but he was able to compare the general mortality rates, infant mortality rates and heights and weights of children of different ages in three areas of York, distinguished according to the proportions living below his poverty line and compared with the servant-keeping classes. The Rowntree family founded the famous chocolate company. They were, and still are, a Quaker family with a great social conscience as shown through the Joseph Rowntree Foundation and Trust.

I simply said to him that he should seek expert medical help and he died laughing!

PATIENT UK

The National Health Service

A Government document in 1944 stated 'One of the fundamental principles of the National Health Service is to divorce the care of health from questions of personal means or other factors irrelevant to it'.

Social capital is a term used for how connected people are to their communities through work, family, membership of clubs, faith groups, and political and social organisations

Aneurin Bevan convinced the Treasury to fund the incredibly expensive package of the NHS in 1948, at a time of post-war austerity and massive nationalisation by the Labour Government, with the argument that a national health service, free at the point of access, would so improve the health of the nation that the percentage of GDP spent on health would diminish. He was succeeded by Enoch Powell as Minister of Health after a general election. He found that there is no limit to the amount of money that could be spent on a national health service. It is a bottomless pit.

Causes of health inequalities

The relationship between social class and what are now called health inequalities is clear from simple observation. They affect not just adults but children too. The reason why they occur merits discussion.

⇨ The question of *post hoc ergo propter hoc* (chicken or the egg) asks if it is the low social class that has led to the poor health or if poor health has led to a deterioration of social status. Studies of the Black Caribbean population in the UK patients found higher rates of psychopathology which were related to socioeconomic disadvantage. However, most chronic diseases tend to present rather later in life, well into adulthood and after careers have been decided and the association with social class is not found. Hence, even looking at the question from the opposite direction and suggesting that the healthy will tend to rise through the social classes does not seem feasible.

⇨ The material explanation blames poverty, poor housing conditions, lack of resources in health and educational provision, as well as higher-risk occupations, for the poor health of the lower social classes. Poverty is demonstrably bad for health. Life expectancy is low in poorer, less-developed countries but the diseases that afflict the developed world tend to be related to obesity and tobacco and injudicious consumption of alcohol. Within the wealthy nations we find that they are most prevalent in their poorest regions and the lower social classes.

⇨ The cultural explanation suggests that the lower social classes prefer less healthy lifestyles, eat more fatty foods, smoke more and exercise less than the middle and upper classes. They have less money to spend on a healthy diet, although this is probably rather less important than a lack of knowledge of what is a healthy diet. People who have been on their feet all day in shops or factories are less likely than office workers to seek activity in the evening, although their daily work has not been adequate to exercise the cardiorespiratory system. Despite the phrase 'as drunk as a lord', the association between binge drinking and social class has been readily noted and Frederich Engels wrote that 'Drink is the bane of the working classes'. Oscar Wilde inverted this to 'Work is the bane of the drinking classes'. Before the first report on smoking and health by the Royal College of Physicians, there was little difference in the incidence of smoking between social classes. Now there is a distinct gradation across social classes. It may seem reasonable to suggest that, when money is short, the first place for economies should be in the consumption of alcohol and tobacco but surveys have shown that in times of economic recession, there is no decline in demand. There is evidence that risk behaviours are unevenly distributed between the social classes and that this contributes to the health gradient. Health is also better in those of higher intelligence as measured by IQ but this does not account for all of the disparity. The West of Scotland Twenty-07 cohort study found that IQ was the second highest risk factor for poor health in socially-deprived communities.

⇨ Social capital is a term used for how connected people are to their communities through work, family, membership of clubs, faith groups, and political and social organisations. This has also been shown to have an impact on health. During the 1950s and 1960s a study of the Italian-American community of Roseto, Pennsylvania, where heart attacks were 50% less frequent than in surrounding communities, explained these differences by the greater social cohesion of this group. This concept has been confirmed by other workers. The idea that social isolation is bad for health is also supported by self-report studies that show housewives, the unemployed and the retired as reporting significantly poorer health than those who are employed.

Addressing the problem

In the past, the major contributory factors to poor health were poor sanitation and infectious diseases. Today the problems relate to smoking, diet and accidents. Alcohol

PATIENT UK

continues to contribute. Diet problems have changed from calorie deficiency to calorie excess.

Social class is not simply a matter of income. A plumber probably earns rather more than a priest but the latter is likely to have the healthier life. The difference in health between social classes is not simply a matter of disposable income.

At the time of writing, the Coalition Government is dismantling the previous administration's 'command and control' approach to public health and is proposing the establishment of local health and wellbeing boards. These would be inclusive organisations involving all the key players in the local health economy, including local authorities, GP commissioners and providers of both primary and secondary care. They would be given a budget and charged with the responsibility to identify and address local public health needs, including health inequalities.

The Coalition's policy on public health is based largely on the Marmot Review *Fair Society, Healthy Lives*. The finer details of the Government's policy on public health issues have yet to be determined but the main principles are enshrined in its White Paper *Healthy Lives, Healthy People*, as follows:

➪ It is important to build people's self-esteem, confidence and resilience right from infancy – with stronger support for early years. Self-esteem is the key to motivating individuals and addressing lifestyle factors that lead to health inequalities. There will be continued commitment to reduce child poverty, an increase in health visitors and a refocusing of the Sure Start scheme.

➪ Preventative services will be focused on delivering the best outcomes for citizens and the emphasis will be on local empowerment initiatives rather than top-down regulations ('the Big Society').

➪ Local government and local communities will be at the heart of improving health and wellbeing for their populations and tackling inequalities. There will be a new integrated public health service – Public Health England.

➪ The Department of Health will publish documents in 2011 on mental health, tobacco control, obesity, sexual health, pandemic flu preparedness, health protection and emergency preparedness and the wider determinants of health.

➪ The Marmot Review identified that people living in the poorest areas die on average seven years earlier than people living in richer areas and spend up to 17 more years living with poor health. They have higher rates of mental illness, of harm from alcohol, drugs and smoking, and of childhood emotional and behavioural problems. Although

deaths from infections are becoming increasingly rare, tuberculosis, sexually transmitted diseases and pandemic flu remain continued threats.

➪ There will be new initiatives to tackle unemployment.

➪ Communities will be designed for 'active ageing' and sustainable growth, with protection of green spaces and encouragement of local food production.

➪ There will be working collaboratively with business and the voluntary sector through a 'Public Health Responsibility Deal' with five networks on food, alcohol, physical activity, health at work and behavioural change.

Last updated: 8 February 2011

EMIS is grateful to Dr Laurence Knott for writing this article. The final copy has passed scrutiny by the independent Mentor GP reviewing team. © EMIS 2011.

➪ The above information is an extract from Patient UK's article *Health and Social Class*, and is reprinted with permission. Visit www.patient.co.uk for more information or to view references for this piece.

© Patient UK

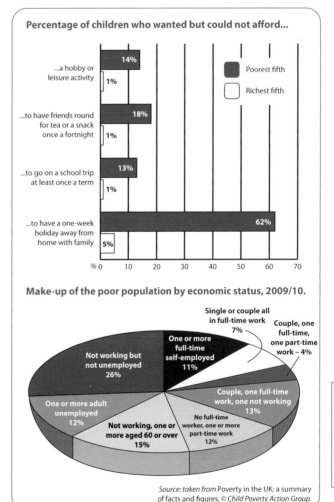

Percentage of children who wanted but could not afford...

- ...a hobby or leisure activity: Poorest fifth 14%, Richest fifth 1%
- ...to have friends round for tea or a snack once a fortnight: Poorest fifth 18%, Richest fifth 1%
- ...to go on a school trip at least once a term: Poorest fifth 13%, Richest fifth 1%
- ...to have a one-week holiday away from home with family: Poorest fifth 62%, Richest fifth 5%

Make-up of the poor population by economic status, 2009/10.

- Not working but not unemployed 26%
- One or more full-time self-employed 11%
- Single or couple all in full-time work 7%
- Couple, one full-time, one part-time work – 4%
- Couple, one full-time work, one not working 13%
- No full-time worker, one or more part-time work 12%
- Not working, one or more aged 60 or over 15%
- One or more adult unemployed 12%

Source: taken from Poverty in the UK: a summary of facts and figures, © Child Poverty Action Group.

PATIENT UK

Social mobility 'slower than in medieval England'

Information from politics.co.uk.

By Ian Dunt

The rate of social mobility in the UK is now slower than during the medieval ages, according to new research.

Researchers at the University of California found that it takes longer for a family's economic and social status to change since the Industrial Revolution than it did during earlier periods of human history.

'The huge social resources spent on publicly-provided education and health have seemingly created no gains in the rate of social mobility,' said Professor Gregory Clark.

'The modern meritocracy is no better at achieving social mobility than the medieval oligarchy'

'The modern meritocracy is no better at achieving social mobility than the medieval oligarchy. Instead that rate seems to be a constant of social physics, beyond the control of social engineering.'

Academics traced the fortunes of people with a rare surname – one rich, the other poor – from 1858-87 to now.

The holders of the 'rich' surname are still 'substantially wealthier' in 2011, four generations later, than the holders of the 'poor' surname.

They also lived an average of three years longer – a good indicator of socio-economic status.

The researchers found that at the current rate of convergence, the groups would not be equal until another two to four generations had passed.

That contrasts negatively with the convergence of groups much earlier in British history.

From the Domesday Book in 1086 until recently, academics found that English society showed 'complete long-run social mobility', meaning there were no permanent classes of rich or poor.

Those bearing the name 'Smith', for example, are mainly descended from the simple village blacksmiths of England in 1350.

By 1450, three or four generations later, the share of 'Smiths' at Oxford equalled their share in the general population. By 1650 there were as many 'Smiths' in the top one per cent of wealth holders as in the general population, indicating that that group had been fully absorbed into the elite.

4 April 2011

⇨ The above information is reprinted with kind permission from politics.co.uk.

© politics.co.uk

How fair is the route to the top?

This article examines trends in people's perceptions of social mobility, factors perceived to be important for getting ahead in Britain, and views about actual and ideal pay levels.

By Anthony Heath, Nan Dirk de Graaf and Yaojun Li

More people think they have been upwardly mobile (that they have a job that is 'higher' up the occupational scale than their father's) than think they have moved downwards.

⇨ 39% think that they are in a higher or much higher job than their father's, while only 23% think they are in a lower or much lower job.

⇨ Long-range mobility is quite rare; people tend to say their jobs are 'higher' or 'lower' than their father's (rather than 'much higher' or 'much lower').

⇨ There has recently been a slight fall in perceived long-range upward mobility. 12% say their job is much higher than their father's, compared with 18% in 1992, and 16% in 1987.

Meritocratic factors are seen as being the most important when it comes to a person 'getting ahead' in modern Britain.

⇨ 84% say hard work is important; 74% a good education; 71% ambition.

⇨ A third (33%) think knowing the right people is important.

⇨ The importance of 'ascriptive factors' (which people are born with or into) has fallen. Being born into a wealthy family was thought to be important by 21% in 1987, but only 14% in 2009. In 1987, 16% thought a person's race/ethnicity was important, compared with 8% in 2009.

People accurately estimate the earnings of those at the lower end of the pay scale, but underestimate the earnings of jobs at the upper end. For example:

⇨ People estimate a shop worker earns £12,000, almost equal to the real average salary of someone with this job.

⇨ Cabinet ministers are estimated to earn £85,000, far lower than their actual salary (£144,500 in 2009).

Generally people believe that wages across the scale are unfair. Those at the bottom of the pay scale are seen to earn less than they should, while those at the top are seen to earn too much.

⇨ On average, people think a shop worker earns £12,000, but believe someone doing this job should earn £16,000. Factory workers are estimated to earn £13,000, but it is thought that they should earn £16,000.

⇨ For example, the chairman of a large company is estimated to earn £200,000, but people feel they should earn £100,000. Cabinet ministers are estimated to earn £85,000, while people feel they should earn £60,000.

Estimates of wages at the top of the pay scale have risen since 1999.

⇨ In 2009 a chairman of a large company was estimated to earn 15 times more than an unskilled factory worker, up from 13 times in 1999.

⇨ However, people think that a chairman of a large company should earn only six times more than an unskilled factory worker, and this has remained unchanged since 1999.

British Social Attitudes 27th Report: find out more at www.natcen.ac.uk
December 2010

⇨ The above information is reprinted with kind permission from NatCen. Visit www.natcen.ac.uk for more information.

© NatCen

NATCEN

Pitfalls on the path to social mobility

Information from the Institute for Fiscal Studies.

By Claire Crawford, Paul Johnson and Anna Vignoles

This Government, alongside most of its predecessors, is concerned about social mobility. A society in which one's prospects are largely or wholly determined by chance of birth is not one with which many will feel comfortable. But any strategy to increase social mobility must be long term, multi-faceted and cautious in its claims.

As the Coalition Government prepares to launch its own strategy for tackling social mobility, recent work at IFS exploring the literature on social mobility has highlighted some important conclusions that the Government would be wise to bear in mind.

First, countries with higher income inequality tend to have lower social mobility (at least when using income-based definitions of mobility). In an unequal society there is further to travel to get from the bottom to the middle or the top. The UK has relatively high income inequality and low social mobility. It is therefore likely to be very hard to increase social mobility without tackling inequality.

> *Continuing to increase the supply of graduates and highly-skilled workers has the potential to reduce wage inequality (or at least slow down increases) and therefore help (in relative terms) those at the bottom*

Particularly in a context of high levels of inequality such as that in the UK, it is important to be clear what one is trying to achieve through increased social mobility. It is obvious that pursuing relative social mobility implies downward mobility for individuals from rich/middle income families. In a world in which the consequences of downward social mobility are significant, there will be many who find this mobility very uncomfortable.

It also matters whether the Government is more concerned about improving the mobility of the most disadvantaged or those somewhat further up the social spectrum. Policies aimed at improving the mobility of the most disadvantaged or the least skilled can be very costly. In part this is because the UK labour market appears to be 'hollowing out', by which we mean there are increasing numbers of high skill and low skill jobs, and fewer in the middle. So it may be harder and more costly to help those at the very bottom than it will be to help those somewhat above the bottom. Any comprehensive social mobility strategy is likely to want to deal with both of these groups and may need to treat them quite differently.

One set of interventions which we know are important are those aimed at very young children, as the recent Field Review and Allen Review have highlighted. But it is equally important to understand that they will never be enough by themselves. The evidence is clear that early investments are most productive if they are followed up with later investments. Important findings in this area are that:

⇨ Continuing to increase the supply of graduates and highly-skilled workers has the potential to reduce wage inequality (or at least slow down increases) and therefore help (in relative terms) those at the bottom.

⇨ Cognitive skills are highly valued in the labour market, and basic skills such as literacy and numeracy have higher economic returns in the UK than in many other countries. But effective interventions in adulthood that improve cognitive skills are not easily found.

⇨ There is emerging evidence that later inventions targeted at improving non-cognitive skills (such as time management, teamwork, leadership skills, self-awareness and even self-control) may be more effective. Certainly there is clear evidence that such non-cognitive skills are highly valued in the labour market.

⇨ Finally, interventions that change students' decisions at key points (e.g. the decision about whether to stay in full-time education beyond age 16), rather than their skills directly, could still have a positive impact on education outcomes and hence social mobility. These will be most productive where they also increase subsequent educational attainment.

April 2011

⇨ The above information is reprinted with kind permission from the Institute for Fiscal Studies. Visit www.ifs.org.uk for more information or to view the original article, which is available free of charge.

© Institute for Fiscal Studies

INSTITUTE FOR FISCAL STUDIES

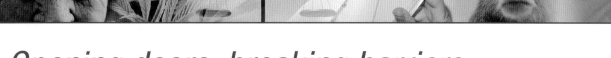

Opening doors, breaking barriers

A strategy for social mobility – executive summary.

A fair society is an open society, one in which every individual is free to succeed. That is why improving social mobility is the principal goal of the Government's social policy.

No one should be prevented from fulfilling their potential by the circumstances of their birth. What ought to count is how hard you work and the skills and talents you possess, not the school you went to or the jobs your parents did. This strategy sets out our vision of a socially mobile country, and how it can become a reality.

There is a long way to go. The income and social class of parents continue to have a huge bearing on a child's chances.

⇨ Only one in five young people from the poorest families achieve five good GCSEs, including English and maths, compared with three-quarters from the richest families.[1]

⇨ 25% of children from poor backgrounds fail to meet the expected attainment level at the end of primary school, compared to 3% from affluent backgrounds.[2]

⇨ Almost one in five children receive free school meals, yet this group accounts for fewer than one in a hundred Oxbridge students.[3]

⇨ Only a quarter of boys from working-class backgrounds get middle-class (professional or managerial) jobs.[4]

⇨ Just one in nine of those with parents from low-income backgrounds reach the top income quartile, whereas almost half of those with parents in the top income quartile stay there.[5]

⇨ Only 7% of the population attend independent schools, but the privately-educated account for more than half of the top level of most professions, including 70% of high court judges, 54% of top journalists and 54% of chief executive officers of FTSE 100 companies.[6]

⇨ The influence of parental income on the income of children in Britain is among the strongest in the Organisation for Economic Co-operation and Development countries. Parental income has over one and a half times the impact on male incomes in Britain compared with Canada, Germany and Sweden.[7]

The lack of social mobility is damaging for individuals. It also leaves the country's economic potential unfulfilled.

This strategy sets out our approach. We are taking a long-term view, and focusing on evidence-based policies. We also recognise that this is not just a task for government. Our whole society has a part to play.

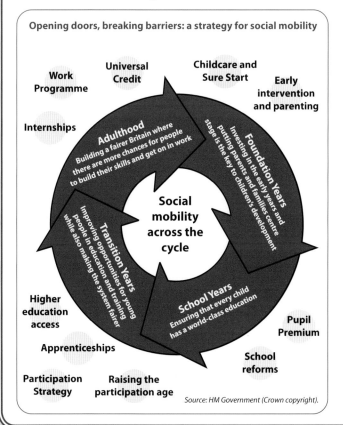

Opening doors, breaking barriers: a strategy for social mobility

Source: HM Government (Crown copyright).

A life cycle approach

Lives are not determined by the age of five, 15 or 30. We know that to make the most of our interventions in the early years, we need to follow through in later life. There should be help and support at every stage to narrow the gaps and provide second chances. That is why our strategy is based on a life cycle framework. Our goal is to make life chances more equal at the critical points for social mobility such as: the early years of development; school readiness at age five; GCSE attainment; the choice of options at 16; gaining a place at university or on an apprenticeship; and getting into and on in the labour market. These are the crucial moments, where we can make the most difference.

Foundation Years

There are already wide variations in ability between children from different backgrounds when they start school. Children at the age of five living in poverty are the equivalent of around eight months behind their peers

in terms of cognitive development.[8] That is why the Foundation Years are such a focus for the Government.

Our Foundation Years approach moves away from a narrow focus on income measures. We have invested in new provision of 15 hours a week of free pre-school education for all disadvantaged two-year-olds, on top of existing provision for all three- and four-year-olds. We are maintaining Sure Start Children's Centres, expanding Family Nurse Partnerships and recruiting thousands more health visitors.

Parents and families have to be centre stage. This strategy sets out plans to support a culture where the key aspects of good parenting are widely understood and where all parents can benefit from advice and support.

School years

Between the ages of five and 16, children develop skills and aspirations that strongly influence their success in further or higher education, and ultimately in the labour market. Children eligible for free school meals are still only half as likely as other children to achieve five good GCSEs, including English and maths,[9] and fewer than 4% achieve the English Baccalaureate.[10] The gaps in achievement between rich and poor actually widen during the school years.[11]

Every child in our country deserves a world-class education. The education system should challenge low aspirations and expectations, dispelling the myth that those from poorer backgrounds cannot aim for top universities and professional careers. Our schools reforms are intended to raise standards across the system, narrow the gaps in attainment and raise aspirations. The Pupil Premium will provide an extra £2.5 billion a year for the most disadvantaged pupils to radically improve their educational outcomes.

This is not just about schools or about government. We can all make a difference to raising aspirations and helping people to make informed choices about jobs and careers. That is why we are launching, with the Education and Employers Taskforce, a drive to get 100,000 people going into schools and colleges to talk about the jobs they do. Every member of the Cabinet has already signed up to speak in schools, and we are encouraging civil servants to use special paid leave to do the same.

Transition years

From 16 onwards, young people's paths diverge sharply. There are many different routes from GCSEs to a job. Choices made during this period of life can have a profound, long-lasting impact.

Too many young people fall out of education and fail to move into employment or training. Over 70,000 16-to 17-year-olds in England, and almost one in five of those aged between 18 and 24, are not in education, employment or training.[12]

And there is sometimes unfairness for those who do remain in education or training. Our vocational system is simply not up to scratch. Access to the most selective universities is too restricted to those from the most privileged backgrounds.[13]

We are improving opportunities for young people in education and training and making the system fairer. The participation age will be raised to 18 by the end of the Parliament, providing over 60,000 extra learning places. Funding for disadvantaged 16- to 19-year-olds in learning will increase by more than a third to £770 million in 2011/12. We are also providing funding to create more than 360,000 new apprenticeships at all ages in 2011/12.

Our reforms to higher education funding put new obligations on universities to improve access. In particular, those universities charging over £6,000 will have to attract more students from less affluent backgrounds.

Too many young people also struggle to get a foothold in the labour market. This is not a new phenomenon – but we are determined to do better. Later this year we will be publishing a strategy setting out how we will improve the participation of young people in education and employment.

Adulthood

Getting on in work should be about merit, not background. Too many struggle to get on in the labour market, held back by low qualifications or a welfare system that does not sufficiently incentivise work. Too many do not get the vital second chances they deserve.

Our welfare reforms will improve work incentives. The Work Programme will tackle the blight of worklessness. We are improving access to education in later life. And for the first time, part-time university students will be entitled to a loan for tuition on the same basis as full-time students.

We need to ensure that the jobs market is fair all the way up to the very top. Success should be based on what you do, not who you know. A large number of the professions remain dominated by a small section of society.[14] Moreover, the independence and security wealth brings is limited to too few.

Employers, and in particular the professions, must play their part in opening up opportunities. Many are already doing so, for example by signing up to a new business compact for fairer, more open internship and work experience programmes.

The Government will lead by example, reforming the civil service, with a new fair and transparent internship

scheme. From 2012 there will be no informal internships in Whitehall.

From strategy to action

We have set ambitious goals for social mobility. Achieving them requires robust mechanisms to underpin the commitments in this strategy. So we are taking steps to ensure: external scrutiny; a new set of leading indicators to help us track progress; and ministerial activity to ensure social mobility is and remains at the heart of our policy agenda.

First, we are creating a new statutory Social Mobility and Child Poverty Commission. The Commission will assess progress on both social mobility and child poverty, holding the Government and others to account and acting as an advocate for change.

Children eligible for free school meals (FSM) are around half as likely as others to get five good GCSEs (five grade A*-C including English and Maths)

31%

58%

FSM

Non-FSM

Source: HM Government (Crown copyright).

Second, we are publishing indicators of progress. Social mobility is by definition a long-term objective. For example, we will only be able to observe the full impact of our Foundation Years policies on social mobility in the 2040s, when the under-threes of today begin to reach their full potential in the labour market. However, there are indicators that we can use to estimate progress over a shorter time frame. This strategy identifies seven key indicators that we will use to track progress. And, for the first time, as departments develop new policies, they will need to consider their impact on social mobility.

These indicators will be included in departmental business plans, ensuring they are at the centre of the work of departments.

Third, the Deputy Prime Minister will continue to chair a group of key Ministers to maintain the momentum for change.

This social mobility strategy is just the beginning. It sets out a clear commitment to improving social mobility, identifies and explains the key decisions we have already taken and announces some further steps. But we do not pretend we have all the answers. Creating an open, fair society will be the work of many parliaments, and the work of the whole nation. But this Government is determined to play its part.

References

1   Gregg P and Goodman A, *Poorer Children's educational attainment: how important are attitudes and behaviours?*, Joseph Rowntree Foundation (2010).

2   Ibid.

3   Sutton Trust, *Responding to the New Landscape for University Access* (2010).

4   Buxton J et al, The long shadow of childhood: associations between parental social class and own social class, educational attainment and timing of first birth; results from the Office for National Statistics Longitudinal Study, *Population Trends 2005* 121:17–26 (2005).

5   Blanden J and Machin S, *Recent Changes in Intergenerational Mobility in Britain*, Sutton Trust (2007).

6   Sutton Trust, *The Educational Backgrounds of Leading Lawyers, Journalists, Vice Chancellors, Politicians, Medics and Chief Executives* (2009).

7   Blanden J, *How Much Can We Learn from International Comparisons of Intergenerational Mobility?*, Centre for the Economics of Education Discussion Paper III (2009).

8   Gregg P and Goodman A, *Poorer Children's educational attainment: how important are attitudes and behaviours?*, Joseph Rowntree Foundation (2010).

9   Department for Education, *GCSE and Equivalent Attainment by Pupil Characteristics in England 2009/10*, Statistical First Release (2010).

10 Department for Education, *The Importance of Teaching: The Schools White Paper* (2010).

11 Gregg P and Goodman A, *Poorer Children's educational attainment: how important are attitudes and behaviours?*, Joseph Rowntree Foundation (2010).

12 Department for Education, *NEET Statistics – Quarterly Brief Labour Force Survey Q4 2010* (2011).

13 Hoare A and Johnston R, *Widening participation through admissions policy – a British case study of school and university performance*, Studies in Higher Education 36(1) (2011).

14 Sutton Trust, *The Educational Backgrounds of Leading Lawyers, Journalists, Vice Chancellors, Politicians, Medics and Chief Executives* (2009).

April 2011

⇨ The above information is an extract from HM Government's report *Opening Doors, Breaking Barriers*, and is reprinted with permission. Visit www.dpm.cabinetoffice.gov.uk for more information on this and other related topics.

© Crown copyright

HM GOVERNMENT

Clegg targets unpaid internships

Lib Dem leader launches strategy to open up career chances, claiming career progression should be less dependent on 'who your father's friends are'. By Allegra Stratton.

The Government is aiming to reverse the growing culture of unpaid internships, which favour the wealthy and well-connected, as part of a social mobility strategy to be launched by Nick Clegg.

The national internship scheme will ask firms to pay young people doing work experience and warn they could otherwise risk a legal challenge under the national minimum wage legislation. The Deputy Prime Minister will say that the aim is to make career progression less dependent on 'who your father's friends are'.

The Conservative party chair, Lady Warsi, will announce on Tuesday that the civil service will end informal internships before 2012. They will all then be advertised on the Government's website.

As one part of a many-pronged effort to narrow differences in achievement between social groups, a number of firms have been enlisted to give people without family connections experience in competitive fields of work. The Government will encourage firms to use name-blank and school-blank applications.

The Government will signal that legislation on the payment of the national minimum wage should be taken more seriously. People will be encouraged to blow the whistle on unpaid internships.

APPLICANTS WHO ATTENDED THE RIGHT SCHOOLS AND HAVE THE RIGHT CONNECTIONS COME THROUGH. ALL OTHERS WAIT HERE.

In advance of the strategy's launch, Clegg and Iain Duncan Smith, the Work and Pensions Secretary, say in a joint article in today's *Telegraph* that many families are seeing their aspirations for their children dashed because private education is out of their reach and they lack the right connections.

Along with pledging to improve social mobility among those from poorer backgrounds, they say that millions of middle-income parents are also not rich enough to insulate their children against life's misfortunes.

'We want a society in which success is based on what you know, not who you know or which family you are born into,' they write. 'So our social mobility drive is aimed at helping the majority of people to move up the rungs of the ladder of opportunity.'

Denying suggestions that the strategy will involve 'social engineering', they cast their drive to open up internships as a way of preventing 'the lucky few grabbing all the best chances'.

'This is mobility for the middle, not just the bottom,' they add.

Research shows that in Britain the influence of parental income on earnings is among the strongest in the OECD. Parental income has more than 1.5 times the impact on male earnings in Britain than in Canada, Germany or Sweden.

The strategy is expected to include seven annual indicators to help the Government monitor social mobility.

Clegg will say: 'For too long, internships have been the almost exclusive preserve of the sharp-elbowed and the well-connected. Unfair, informal internships can rig the market in favour of those who already have opportunities.

'We want a fair job market based on merit, not networks. It should be about what you know, not who you know.'

Lawyers Allen & Overy; management consultants PWC and KPMG; media groups Channel 4 and the *Guardian*; and the Royal Institute of British Architects have agreed to offer placements and pay the national minimum wage or 'reasonable out-of-pocket expenses' for any work done in their offices.

As part of a 'business compact on social mobility', companies will be required to work with local schools, giving staff time off to mentor children. As a result, 100,000 adults established in their careers should go into schools at least once a year to talk about their work. Firms must also advertise work experience in schools.

20 April 2011

© Guardian News and Media Limited 2011

THE GUARDIAN

Tackling inequality is key to improving social mobility, Mr Clegg

By Duncan Exley, campaign director for One Society.

Today, Nick Clegg launches a Royal Commission on social mobility. There are a number of reasons to celebrate this.

Firstly, because it is necessary. The UK has one of the lowest rates of social mobility in the developed world. This is a tragedy for those 'trapped at the bottom', but also for the rest of us who will not benefit from the contribution of those who never get to become the innovators, teachers, entrepreneurs or surgeons that they could have been.

Secondly, because Nick Clegg is proposing the adoption of social mobility indicators, which include measures – such as birth weight and the proportion of former state school pupils in top universities – that are of real importance in a civilised and productive society.

Also welcome is the commitment to address the growing injustice of unpaid internships, with an indication that companies which continue this practice may 'risk a legal challenge under the national minimum wage legislation'.

On the other hand, statements already made by the Deputy Prime Minister raise serious concerns. Perhaps the most worrying is Nick Clegg's claim that:

'Social mobility is what characterises a fair society, rather than a particular level of income equality.'

It is worrying for a number of reasons.

Firstly, I think most people would question whether the current 'particular level of income inequality' characterises a 'fair society'.

For example, is it fair that the average pay of a Reckitt Benckiser employee in 2009 was 0.07% that of the company's chief executive? Is it fair that the wealth gap between the UK's 10th and 90th percentiles is 1:97? And is it really OK that millions spend their childhood in poverty (sometimes so severe as to reduce life expectancy by decades), as long as some of them eventually climb out?

Secondly, there is overwhelming evidence that the most effective way to increase social mobility is to reduce income inequality (i.e. trying to address social mobility while ignoring inequality is like trying to lose weight but ignoring calories). Study after study after study after study shows that it is 'likely to be very hard to increase social mobility without tackling inequality' and that:

'Income inequality can become entrenched across generations, as elites monopolise top jobs regardless of their talent, gaining preferential access to capital and opportunities. This harms social mobility.'

There are means of encouraging social mobility that do not involve reducing income inequality, including introducing and encouraging the children of low-income parents (and children looked after by the state) to have education and career opportunities beyond their families' experience.

However, social mobility can take generations; it will be a colossal shame if, after a few decades, the indicators that are now being proposed merely tell us that we have spent valuable time tinkering around the edges and neglecting the real driver of social mobility.

7 April 2011

⇨ The above information is reprinted with kind permission from One Society (originally published by Left Foot Forward). Visit www.onesociety.org.uk for more.

© One Society

ONE SOCIETY

Upwardly mobile?

Policies need to be aimed at raising school attainment of children from poorer backgrounds to increase social mobility, says Lindsey MacMillan.

The Coalition recently unveiled its blueprint for improving equality of opportunity in the UK. The Social Mobility Strategy Review was a little light on explicit policy interventions and it is probably too soon to say whether the enthusiasm for improving social mobility will translate into better life chances for children. However, one thing that is clear is how far there is to go to achieving a more equal society.

Measuring mobility takes a long time, as we need to study individuals from childhood through to their adult life. Hence the latest evidence relates to people now aged 41 who were born in 1970. This data found that individuals born to poorer families were more likely to end up the lowest paid as adults than if they had been born to the same circumstances 12 years previously. Social mobility decreased across time in the UK (Blanden, Gregg, Goodman, Machin, 2004).

Following on from this, research found that educational attainment was the main driver of immobility across generations. For the 1970 cohort of sons, family income was more closely related to their educational attainment than in the earlier cohort and this was a key factor in their lower mobility levels (Blanden, Gregg and Macmillan, 2007).

Focusing in on access to the top professions, those who go on to become lawyers and doctors come from substantially richer families than the average individual and this pattern became stronger across time. In contrast, while those who became doctors and lawyers were of higher ability than the average, this trend has weakened across time. This would suggest that there is a widening social gap in entry to the top professions, not driven by ability. While individuals entering top professions in the last decade looked less like the average individual in terms of their family income in childhood, they looked more like the average individual in terms of their ability than the previous cohort (Macmillan, 2009).

All of the evidence mentioned above focuses on individuals now in their 40s and 50s. For people born more recently we cannot yet observe their adult earnings but we can instead look at educational opportunity which is such a strong driver on mobility. A couple of new pieces of work have analysed the link between family background and educational attainment to get a picture of what we might expect for the future. The evidence is mixed.

On the one hand, there is some evidence for children born around 1990 that the association between family incomes, Key Stage 2 attainment and GCSE attainment is weakening, reducing the socio-economic gradient. This could be a promising sign. There is also the suggestion that post-16 participation in education has become less associated with where you come from (Gregg and Macmillan, 2009). On the other hand, there is less evidence of this trend continuing into higher education and no change in the relationship between background and early attainment (age three to five) for children born around 2000 (Blanden and Machin, 2009).

So what can be done? Identifying effective policies in this setting is often problematic. However, some research in the US from the Perry pre-school programme indicates that improving behavioural patterns in early childhood had positive effects in terms of greater employability, less contact with the police and higher completed education levels (Heckman et al, Various). There is also evidence that lower family income in childhood causes lower educational attainment and lower education reduces life chances (Dahl and Lochner [2008], Oreopoulus et al [2006]).

With this view that education is still a key policy lever in changing patterns of mobility, policies need to be aimed at raising school attainment of children from poorer backgrounds. Increasing the numbers that stay on into post-compulsory education and specifically into university will be important in reversing the decline in mobility. The Government has set up a sizeable research fund to work out what causes increased educational attainment of the poorest children as well as the new pupil premium to fund interventions in schools. Unfortunately the most recent policy announcements on the scrapping of the Education Maintenance Allowance and trebling of tuition fees are unlikely to encourage such changes in behaviour.

Lindsey MacMillan is a post-graduate research assistant at the ESRC Centre for Market and Public Organisation. Her work focuses on the economics of the family, including intergenerational mobility, the role of education in mobility, inequality in educational attainment and intergenerational worklessness.

Summer 2011

⇨ The above article first appeared in the Economic and Social Research Council's *Society Now* magazine, and is reprinted with their kind permission. Visit www.esrc.ac.uk for more information.

© *Economic and Social Research Council*

ECONOMIC AND SOCIAL RESEARCH COUNCIL

The gap years: education and social immobility

Despite having been high on the political agenda for decades, the educational gap between rich and poor children is still stark in Britain in 2011. Research shows that a wide range of influences conspire against poor children gaining a good education.

'On the education of the people of this country the fate of the country depends.' This proclamation from Benjamin Disraeli is still shared by today's politicians a century and a half later. Ensure access to a proper education for all, and the result is improved wellbeing, prosperity and social mobility – benefiting both individuals and society in general. Or at least, that has been the ambition.

But although the politicians may be willing, the results are weak – or limited at best. Children growing up in poorer households are still generally underperforming in school. Despite hopes, performance targets and rigorous testing have not propelled ever larger numbers of British children and teenagers up the education ladder.

As research shows, there is no 'silver bullet' to tackle the education challenge. The report *Poorer children's educational attainment: how important are attitudes and behaviour*, by Alissa Goodman at the Institute for Fiscal Studies and Professor Paul Gregg at the ESRC Centre for Market and Public Organisation (CMPO), uses data from several ESRC-funded longitudinal surveys to analyse influences on children's educational attainment. It reveals that a wide range of factors come into play – including not only material resources, but also aspirations and attitudes both from the child and from their parents.

The report, funded by the Joseph Rowntree Foundation, shows that the cracks appear at a very early stage. According to data from the Millennium Cohort Study there are already 'considerable gaps' in cognitive test scores by the age of three between children in the poorest fifth of the population and children from better-off households – and these gaps widen by the age of five. Not only cognitive abilities, but children's social and emotional wellbeing follow a similar development through childhood years.

> **Ironically, once children start school the educational gap does not narrow; it widens more quickly**

One important factor may be the home environment and how much it encourages, or discourages, learning. Results show clear differences between poor and better-off households both in health and wellbeing, family interactions, home learning environment and parenting styles.

'Children from poorer families enter the school system considerably behind those from affluent families. This is associated with a weaker home learning environment and less sensitive parenting,' says Professor Paul Gregg.

Ironically, once children start school the educational gap does not narrow; it widens more quickly. An analysis of the Avon Longitudinal Study of Parents and Children reveals that the gap grows particularly fast during primary school years. Poorer children who performed badly in Key Stage tests at age seven were less likely to improve their ranking compared with better-off children. And even those poorer children who performed well at this age were more likely to fall behind the better-off by age 11.

Only around three-quarters of children from the poorest fifth of families reach the expected Key Stage 2 level at age 11, compared with 97 per cent of children from the richest fifth.

'Throughout the school years bright children from poorer families drift away from educational achievement – through lower aspirations, a lack of belief that their own efforts can lead to academic success, and fewer material resources in the home to support learning, for instance Internet access,' explains Professor Gregg.

Percentage of students from routine/manual occupational backgrounds[1] attending top UK universities[2], 2009/10

University	Percentage
University of Oxford	11.3%
University of Cambridge	10.4%
Imperial College London	17.8%
University College London	17.5%
University of Edinburgh	16.5%
London School of Economics and Political Science	20.7%
University of Manchester	21.3%
King's College London	20.8%
University of Bristol	15.4%
Durham University	12.8%

(% axis: 0, 5, 10, 15, 20, 25)

1. NS-SEC classes 4, 5, 6 and 7.
2. Top 10 UK universities according to The Times Higher Education World University Rankings 2011/12: www.timeshighereducation.co.uk/world-university-rankings/2011-2012/europe.html

Source: HESA Student Record. Taken from Table T1a – Participation of under-represented groups in higher education: young full-time first degree entrants 2009/10 (http://www.hesa.ac.uk/dox/performanceIndicators/0910/t1a_0910.xls). Reproduced by permission of the Higher Education Statistics Agency Limited. HESA cannot accept responsibility for any conclusions or inferences derived from the data by third parties.

ECONOMIC AND SOCIAL RESEARCH COUNCIL

Alissa Goodman and Paul Gregg point to several reasons why poorer children fall ever further behind during primary school – including parents' aspirations for higher education, the belief of parents and children in determining their life course through their own actions, and children's behavioural problems. Findings show that only 37 per cent of the poorest mothers said they hoped their child would go to university, compared with 81 per cent of the richest mothers. 'Such adverse attitudes to education of disadvantaged mothers are one of the single most important factors associated with lower educational attainment at age 11,' the researchers state in their report.

By the time the children finish primary school these gaps are wide and established. Analysis of the Longitudinal Study of Young People in England showed that further widening through teenage years is relatively small in comparison to the childhood years. At this stage it is harder to reverse patterns of under-achievement, but attitudes and aspirations continue to be important factors. Pupils are more likely to do well at GCSEs with a good home environment, parents expecting them to go on to higher education, and access to computers and Internet. Their own attitudes are also crucial, such as a belief in their own abilities, a belief that their actions make a difference, an expectation of applying for and entering higher education, and avoidance of anti-social behaviour.

'These findings suggest that attitudes and behaviour are potentially important links between socio-economic disadvantage and children's educational attainment,' conclude the researchers. They argue that policy measures should target two areas in particular: the home learning environment and parents' aspirations, and the child's own attitudes and behaviours.

Without success in closing the 'education gap' between poorer families and the better-off, true social mobility and an equal society will remain an elusive political goal. As the American educational reformer Horace Mann declared: 'Education, beyond all other devices of human origin, is the great equaliser of the conditions of men – the balance-wheel of the social machinery.'

From the ESRC magazine *Society Now*.

7 April 2011

⇨ The above information is reprinted with kind permission from the Economic and Social Research Council. Visit www.esrc.ac.uk for more information.

© *Economic and Social Research Council*

Involving employers in schools can encourage social mobility

Information from Children & Young People Now.

By Neil Puffett

Increased engagement by employers at school can help address issues of low aspiration and social mobility, a study has found.

A report by Deloitte, commissioned by charity the Education and Employers Taskforce, examined how employers can contribute to improving careers education through inspiring and better informing young people.

It found that 95 per cent of young people agreed that they would like employers to be more involved in providing advice and guidance about careers and jobs.

In the past two years, 42 per cent of those surveyed said they had no contact with employers at all, and 40 per cent had contact with between one and four employers.

The study found that young people who had been in contact with four or more employers in the past two years of school were nearly twice as likely to believe that they had a good idea of the knowledge and skills needed for the jobs they wanted to do.

David Cruickshank, Deloitte chairman and trustee at the Education and Employers Taskforce, said: 'This report shows the importance of employers playing an active part in the school curriculum, and critically that this is recognised by schools, employers and by young people themselves.

'The involvement of employers, when done properly, motivates, inspires and informs young people, and prepares them for the workplace by making them aware of the skills and attitudes employers expect them to have.

'At a time when there is considerable pressure on public spending, this report shows the positive steps and measures that schools, employers and the Government can take, at little cost, to work together to overcome these barriers and instil careers education into the curriculum.'

8 October 2010

⇨ The above information is reprinted with kind permission from Children & Young People Now. Visit www.cypnow.co.uk for more information.

© *Children & Young People Now*

ECONOMIC AND SOCIAL RESEARCH COUNCIL / CHILDREN & YOUNG PEOPLE NOW

Children's education crucial for social mobility

Educational inequalities may be reduced by policies focused on parents and the family home, and children's own attitudes and behaviours.

Key findings

⇨ The early home learning environment and emerging behaviour, attitudes and beliefs influenced by family background are important long-term factors for how well children perform in school.

⇨ Mothers' aspirations for higher education and children's behavioural problems stand out as particularly important during the primary school years. 81 per cent of the richest mothers say they hope their nine-year-old will go to university, compared with only 37 per cent of the poorest mothers.

⇨ The gap between children from richer and poorer backgrounds, already large at age five, continues to widen between ages five and 14.

⇨ By age 11, only around three quarters of children from the poorest fifth of families reach the Government's expected level at Key Stage 2, compared to 97 per cent of children from the richest fifth.

⇨ In later years patterns of under-achievement become harder to reverse – but influential factors are: expectations for higher education, access to a computer and the Internet, teenagers' experiences of bullying, anti-social behaviour and behavioural problems at school.

⇨ Only 21 per cent of the poorest fifth (measured by parental socioeconomic position) manage to gain five good GCSEs, compared to 75 per cent of the top quintile – a gap of an astonishing 54 percentage points.

Background

It is well known that children growing up in poor families emerge from UK schools with substantially lower levels of educational attainment. Since educational qualifications are such a strong determinant of later-life income and opportunities, such achievement gaps are a major contributing factor to patterns of poverty and social immobility.

This research considers some of the ways that affluence and disadvantage influence children's educational attainment. It focuses on a broad set of aspirations, attitudes and behaviours varying across childhood.

In order to study these factors, data have been taken from several longitudinal studies including the Millennium Cohort Study, the Avon Longitudinal Study of Parents and Children, and the British Cohort Study. The children

in these studies have been observed at various points in time from early childhood through to late adolescence.

The findings suggest that the aspirations, attitudes and behaviours of parents and children potentially have an important part to play in explaining why poor children typically do worse at school.

Policy relevance and implications

The research evidence shows two major areas where policy might help to reduce educational inequalities:

Parents and the family home

⇨ Improving the home learning environment in poorer families (e.g. books and reading pre-school, computers in teenage years).

⇨ Helping parents from poorer families to believe that their own actions and efforts matter.

⇨ Raising families' aspirations and desire for advanced education, from primary school onwards.

The child's own attitudes and behaviours

⇨ Reducing children's behavioural problems and engagement in risky behaviours.

⇨ Helping children from poorer families to believe that their own actions and efforts matter.

⇨ Raising children's aspirations and desire for advanced education, from primary school onwards.

Some of the outlined measures appear better covered by existing policy and research evidence than others. For example:

⇨ There is much less emphasis on parenting programmes and improving child behaviours in primary and secondary school, compared with pre-school years, although our research suggests that reaching families while children are of school age might continue to be useful.

⇨ Intensive programmes that focus on children most in need tend to have the strongest evidence base behind them, but policy might need to focus more on the larger number of children from low-income families with lower intensity than those at the extreme.

⇨ Programmes to raise educational aspirations typically start in the secondary school years, while our research suggests that such interventions would be worthwhile at a younger age.

ECONOMIC AND SOCIAL RESEARCH COUNCIL

Brief description of the research

The report *Poorer children's educational attainment: how important are attitudes and behaviour?* considers some of the ways that affluence and disadvantage influence children's educational attainment. It is available at www.jrf.org.uk/publications/educational-attainment-poor-children

The report was funded by the Joseph Rowntree Foundation and was carried out by the ESRC research centre CMPO, and the IFS which hosts an ESRC centre.

20 June 2011

⇨ The above information is reprinted with kind permission from the Economic and Social Research Council. Visit www.esrc.ac.uk for more information.

© *Economic and Social Research Council*

Academies will struggle to break public schools' grip on top jobs

'Meritocracy died at the end of the last century. Rest in peace.'

By Calum Benson

Education policies of recent decades came under sustained fire last night as Andrew Neil lamented the demise of grammar schools, something he linked to the increasing domination of politics by 'old boys' from the country's most élite public schools.

Whatever your politics, it was hard not to feel slightly disheartened hearing Jacob Rees-Mogg, old Etonian and Tory MP for North-East Somerset, say in all sincerity: 'I am a man of the people. *Vox populi, vox dei.*' (That's 'the voice of the people is the voice of God', to the rest of us).

Neil is not alone in worrying. James Groves, head of the education unit at the Policy Exchange think tank, thinks that Neil does have 'a very fair point'.

Unless academies surprise many observers and do re-light the fires of social mobility, a debate on academic selection may not be as distant as it has often seemed

Others remain unconvinced. A spokesperson for the ATL teaching union said that social mobility was the wrong priority, commenting that it infers 'some people going up the ladder, and some people coming down'. They point to other causes for Neil's problem, saying it shows 'how closed those professions have become'.

The programme comes at a topical moment. Neil neglected to mention the Government's academy programme, designed to free schools from the interference and prescription of local authority. The brainchild of Andrew Adonis and adopted by the Coalition, academies have today been credited by the cross-party Public Accounts Committee report with having 'improved pupils' life chances in some of the most deprived communities in the country.'

But whether they can introduce a new meritocracy is less certain. The Department of Education declined to comment on the issues raised in Neil's programme, careful not to ascribe such lofty aspirations to the academies system.

Anastasia de Waal, Head of Family and Education at Civitas, is unconvinced. Speaking to Total Politics this afternoon, she said that the key to social mobility is: 'a comprehensive "elite" education... where all young people have access to the same curriculum'. This is something that academies have thus far failed to deliver, she feels. Rather, they encourage 'a scenario in which pupils from lower-income backgrounds are routed into an alternative curriculum'.

Groves believes academies are a step in the right direction, lauding them as a 'great improvement' on the comprehensive system. However, he remained cautious, saying only that they can provide great opportunities for students.

For many parents though, 'can' is not guarantee enough. Unless academies surprise many observers and do re-light the fires of social mobility, a debate on academic selection may not be as distant as it has often seemed, despite the level of political toxicity that has hung over it since the abolishment of most state grammar schools.

27 January 2011

⇨ This article originally appeared on the Total Politics website www.totalpolitics.com/blog and is reprinted with their kind permission.

© *Total Politics*

Class has much bigger effect on white pupils' results

Poverty has a much greater influence on how White British pupils do at school than it does on the academic performance of other ethnic groups, two new studies have concluded.

Researchers investigating academic performance in an Inner London borough found that, for pupils from most ethnic minorities, the socio-economic backgrounds of each child's parents had only limited impact on how much progress they made during the last four years of primary school.

However, for White British pupils, the picture was very different, with those from better-off homes pulling away dramatically from their peers from less advantaged backgrounds. This meant that, while White British pupils from well-off families were the top-performing ethnic group at age 11, those eligible for free school meals had among the worst results.

White working class parents might have, on average, lower educational aspirations for their children than those from immigrant groups

Professor Steve Strand, of the University of Warwick, will present the findings at the British Educational Research Association's conference in Warwick today. They come from an investigation into pupil performance in the ethnically diverse South London borough of Lambeth, commissioned by the borough council itself.

Professor Strand says: 'The effects of economic disadvantage are much less pronounced for most minority ethnic groups. Those from low socio-economic backgrounds seem to be much more resilient to the impact of disadvantage than their White British peers.'

The findings are consistent with a new national study, being presented at BERA on Saturday, 4 September. This shows that there is a bigger gap between the GCSE performance of pupils from disadvantaged and non-disadvantaged backgrounds among white teenagers than for any other ethnic group among those categorised.

Some 31 per cent of white pupils eligible for free school meals (FSM) achieved five A*-C GCSE grades, the study found, compared to 63 per cent among those from better-off backgrounds who were not FSM [eligible for free school meals]. This performance gap of 32 percentage points was much higher than that of any of

the other six ethnic groups; for Bangladeshi teenagers, it was only seven points, and for Chinese pupils, only five points.

Establishing why the social class gap is so much bigger for White British pupils than others is not easy. However, Professor Strand says it is likely that White British pupils from well-off families have better access to 'social and economic capital' than their counterparts from other ethnic groups, and that white working class parents might have, on average, lower educational aspirations for their children than those from immigrant groups.

Disadvantage, ethnicity, gender and educational attainment: The case of White working class pupils will be presented by Steve Strand at the BERA conference today (3 September).

3 September 2010

⇨ The above information is reprinted with kind permission from the British Educational Research Association. Visit www.bera.ac.uk for more information.

© *British Educational Research Association*

BRITISH EDUCATIONAL RESEARCH ASSOCIATION

Education isn't a zero-sum game

Information from the Adam Smith Institute.

By Sam Bowman

The Government has been criticised for its new 'idea' for universities, to allow rich students to buy places at university. Students will be able to pay the fees that foreign students pay in order to guarantee a place in the course they want. Isn't this just a sop to the rich that will further harm social mobility? Well, yes and no. It will benefit rich students, but it will open a great many other doors as well.

We are living through a crisis in university education. Last year, 188,697 university applicants failed to get a place after clearing, an increase of around 40% on the year before. This kind of shortage is all too predictable – when you set a price ceiling for something, you should expect shortages. For an example of this, look at the 1973 oil crisis. The US and UK imposed price controls and experienced fuel queues and shortages; Japan and Germany allowed prices to rise and consumption dropped in reaction, with fuel going to the places it was most in demand. So it is with university places – there is more demand than supply, so many people will be left unsatisfied. While this is true of the sector in general, it's also true for specific universities. Demand for Oxbridge and Russell Group universities is far higher than the supply of places.

> **We are living through a crisis in university education. Last year, 188,697 university applicants failed to get a place after clearing, an increase of around 40% on the year before**

The Government's proposals would allow some applicants to pay their own way – creating a place that would otherwise not have existed. This is the crucial point to remember. If a girl's parents pay the extra price for her to go to Oxford, nobody else is deprived of a place. And the place is only available if she has the grades that would qualify her for it anyway. Because the sector is operating under capacity (thanks to the fees price ceiling), paying full fees for a place will create an entirely new place. It's a positive-sum game.

Some say this is unfair because it offers the rich more options than the poor. But to stop people from being able to pay for places just to bring them down to the level of the poor is completely backwards – we should be trying to see how we can raise the poor up to that level. Equality for its own sake shouldn't be the objective; what we want is to improve people's lives. So how could we do this? Quite simply: by making sure that student loans are available to everybody with the grades needed for these places, and allowing universities to raise their fees to reflect the supply and demand for places.

More places would be created and the places lottery would be done away with – if you want to do medicine at Oxford, you'd better be prepared to make the same sacrifices that your competitors are willing to make. The proposals announced today will only entrench privilege if people continue to insist on artificially depressing place numbers through the fees cap.

10 May 2011

⇨ The above information is reprinted with kind permission from the Adam Smith Institute. Visit www.adamsmith.org for more information.

© Adam Smith Institute

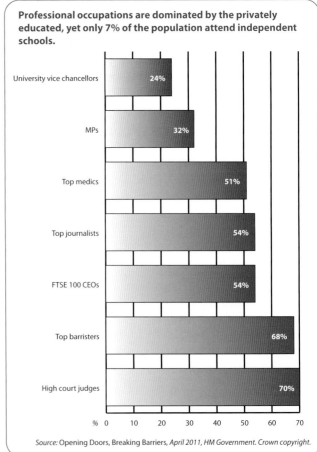

Professional occupations are dominated by the privately educated, yet only 7% of the population attend independent schools.

- University vice chancellors — 24%
- MPs — 32%
- Top medics — 51%
- Top journalists — 54%
- FTSE 100 CEOs — 54%
- Top barristers — 68%
- High court judges — 70%

% 0 10 20 30 40 50 60 70

Source: Opening Doors, Breaking Barriers, April 2011, HM Government. Crown copyright.

THE ADAM SMITH INSTITUTE

Social mobility: a case for grammar schools?

Is the meritocracy of the UK's post-war years finally coming to an end?

Yes, says Andrew Neil from the BBC's *The Politics Show*. In last night's provocative documentary *Posh and Posher: Why Public School Boys Run Britain*, Neil cites statistics which make gloomy reading for social mobility in 21st-century Britain. Many of them you will have heard before. 66% of the Coalition were privately educated. 18 of the 23 full-time Cabinet Ministers are millionaires. According to *The Sunday Times*, David Cameron 'has more Etonians around him than any leader since Macmillan'. Can he really represent Britain, from such a narrow base?

The Conservatives have generally waved away such questions as part of Labour's 'class war', but in private, the Coalition is perhaps more acknowledging of its faults. In *Posh and Posher*, Mr Neil speaks with MPs Sarah Teather and David Davis, who both admit their uneasiness over the current composition of Westminster. 'I think it matters that politicians at the moment don't represent the United Kingdom,' said Teather, the Lib Dem minister at the Education Department. 'I don't think that's a good thing. I don't think it's good for trust in politicians.' David Davis, who grew up on a council estate and was grammar-school educated, was asked by Mr Neil whether someone from his kind of background would today have the same kind of opportunities that he had. 'Oh, no,' he replied, 'no, I don't think so at all.'

Andrew Neil wonders whether the key to meritocracy lies ultimately with academic selection. 'Today's political elite on the left and right is unanimous in opposing the kind of reforms to our state schools that would reignite the meritocratic revolution,' he says. 'As a result, we're likely to be even more governed in the years ahead by a narrow elite – unrepresentative of the kind of people we are.' Are grammar schools, then, the way forward?

This is a national debate that gets reopened once every couple of years, and there are fierce advocates on either side. In 2007, David Cameron refused to back the creation of new grammar schools and got himself into hot water with members of the influential 1922 Committee. He referred to supporters of the grammar school system as 'inverse class warriors', and said the debate was 'entirely pointless'. The incident has become known, predictably, as 'grammarsgate'. The proponents of a three-tier education system – including, it would seem, Andrew Neil – have argued that grammar schools were successfully meritocratic, and that social mobility has deteriorated since they were phased out.

It's a complex debate, and one that the main parties have tended to shy away from. In 2000, Education Secretary David Blunkett said he was 'desperately trying to avoid the whole debate in education concentrating on the issue of selection' saying that 'arguments about selection are a past agenda'. It was a Labour Government which abolished the tripartite system back in 1976, and a cohort of MPs in the party has opposed academic selection ever since.

Indeed, the very idea of selection is ringed with problems. Critics argue that the 11-plus is an unreliable and divisive means of testing people, which assumes a degree of development that may not yet have been reached. It has been alleged that there is an adverse psychological effect on those who fail. Kent and Lincolnshire, for example, both operate selective systems, and although their grammar school results are typically above average, both counties have a high proportion of schools in the National Challenge – i.e. schools where fewer than 30% of the students achieve five GCSE grades A* to C. Kent, in fact, has more National Challenge schools than any local education authority in England.

There's also a big problem with the main thrust of Neil's argument: that grammar schools are somehow better for social mobility. With only a fraction of students being entitled to free school meals, the intake for most grammar schools is firmly middle class. In fact, according to 2008 research, half of children at grammar schools were sent to private tutors to pass the entrance test.

Like Neil, Davis and Peter Mandelson, I attended a grammar school: Bourne Grammar School, a small, mixed-gender school in south Lincolnshire. It's a quiet, sheltered, high-achieving school and I enjoyed my time there. Indeed, had I not gone there, I doubt I would have done as well in my GCSEs and A-Levels or been fortunate enough to attend a world-class university. But that doesn't mean the grammar school system itself is good for social mobility.

Going back to selective schools seems like too simplistic a solution. Grammar schools don't get rid of social elitism; if anything, they stratify intake even further. There might be more opportunities for the bright and 'un-monied', but those who aren't high achievers could end up doing worse than they would in a comprehensive system. Neil is right to observe a decline in social mobility and post-war meritocracy, but to lay the blame at the feet of the 1975 Labour Government seems more than a little simplistic.

27 January 2011

⇨ Information from Political Reboot. Visit www.politicalreboot.co.uk for more.

© *Political Reboot*

POLITICAL REBOOT

Higher education outcomes

Comprehensive pupils outperform independent and grammar pupils in university degrees.

Students from comprehensive schools are likely to achieve higher-class degrees at university than independent- and grammar-school students with similar A-Levels and GCSE results, a major study commissioned by the Sutton Trust and the Government shows. This is one of the main findings from a five-year study by the National Foundation for Educational Research tracking 8,000 A-Level students to investigate whether the US-based SAT could be used in university admissions in the UK.

A comprehensive-school student with A-Level grades BBB, for example, is likely to perform as well in their university degree as an independent- or grammar-school student with A-Level grades ABB or AAB – i.e. one to two grades higher. Comprehensive-school pupils also performed better than their similarly qualified independent- and grammar-school counterparts in degrees from the most academically selective universities and across all degree classes, awarded to graduates in 2009.

The final report from the study published today concludes that the SAT results are a poorer predictor of degree results than A-Levels or GCSEs, and that the test does not identify academic potential among disadvantaged pupils that might be missed by A-Levels.

Sir Peter Lampl, Chairman of the Sutton Trust, said: 'These findings provide further evidence that universities are right to take into account the educational context of students when deciding whom to admit – alongside other information on their achievements and potential.

'We are obviously disappointed that the SAT does not provide an extra tool in helping to identify academic talent among students from less-privileged homes – but this study does at least demonstrate the need for all university admissions tests to be properly evaluated in this way. One issue has been that during the last five years the SAT has become less of an aptitude test and more of an achievement test similar to A-Levels.'

The study found that comprehensive-school students, who achieve the same level of degree as students from an independent or grammar school (with the same GCSE attainment and other background characteristics), are likely to have an average A-Level grade that is approximately 0.5 to 0.7 of a grade lower.

These differences emerge for all types of universities, including the most academically selective universities – despite the fact that a greater proportion of grammar- and independent-school pupils end up at these institutions. The study took into account the fact that some universities demand higher A-Level grades for entry than others. The final report focuses on the degree results of 2,750 students who graduated in 2009.

> **'Universities are right to take into account the educational context of students when deciding whom to admit'**

The study concludes that the SAT has some power to predict degree outcomes but it does not add any additional information, over and above that provided by GCSEs and A-Levels (or GCSEs alone), at a significantly useful level. It finds no evidence that the SAT provides sufficient information to identify students with the potential to benefit from higher education whose ability is not adequately reflected in their A-Levels or GCSEs. Meanwhile, the SAT was found not to distinguish between the most able university applicants, for example those who get three or more A grades at A-Level.

Notes

This is the final report of a five-year research study, co-funded by the Department for Business, Innovation and Skills (BIS), the National Foundation for Educational Research (NFER), the Sutton Trust and the College Board, examining the validity of an aptitude test (the SAT) for use in higher education (HE) admissions.

The study aimed to provide information on:

⇨ how the SAT could help predict university outcomes together with A-Levels;

⇨ whether the SAT could distinguish between the most able students who get straight As at A-Level;

⇨ if the SAT could help identify students from disadvantaged backgrounds who may have the potential to benefit from higher education.

3 December 2010

⇨ The above information is reprinted with kind permission from the Sutton Trust. Visit their website at www.suttontrust.com for more information on this and other related topics.

© *Sutton Trust*

SUTTON TRUST

How do disadvantaged children succeed against the odds?

Parent power can help disadvantaged children get ahead. Parents whose children succeed against the odds of social and economic disadvantage 'actively cultivate' their offspring, nurturing their skills and allowing them to benefit from the education system.

By Iram Siraj-Blatchford[1], Aziza Mayo[1], Edward Melhuish[2], Brenda Taggart[1], Pam Sammons[3] and Kathy Sylva[3]

The highly-respected Effective Pre-School, Primary and Secondary Education (EPPSE) 3-16 project has followed the progress of more than 3,000 children since 1997, from the age of three to 16. Its new report on performing against the odds shows how parents, teachers, networks of family and friends and children themselves interact and contribute to young people's success, even when the children are from working class backgrounds.

The research highlights the importance of recruiting the best teachers to schools in disadvantaged communities and demonstrates that additional support classes are crucial for the children in these schools. The researchers also say that schools and communities should provide extra educational experiences for 'vulnerable' children.

They found that teachers who helped these children were able to explain clearly and were approachable when things were difficult to understand. Successful children showed determination and self-belief.

Parents of children who succeed against the odds set and reinforce high standards for behaviour and academic aspirations and explicitly express their high esteem for education. 'Even if parents did not have much money or high levels of education, they strongly believed in their own ability to support their child's learning,' said Iram Siraj-Blatchford of the Institute of Education, London, who led the Department for Education-funded research. 'If they had a gap in their own knowledge, they found others who could help.'

Children who have had this nurturing are primed to make the most of the high-quality pre-schools their parents carefully chose for them when they start school and to carry on doing well. The researchers say that early assessment and a personalised pre-school curriculum could help more children master important school-relevant skills that help them to succeed against the odds.

The research shows that children seen as clever and hard working, with a positive attitude, developed a more positive self-image as learners, which was then constantly reinforced by those at home and school. This positive perception of children's ability was reinforced by the perception of parents and children that 'ability to learn' was something that could be shaped and wasn't a 'given'. 'In contrast, children who experienced learning difficulties or were not seen as particularly clever often developed a negative self-image, resulting in or reinforcing ineffective problem-solving strategies, diminished motivation for school and learning, and a sense of helplessness,' says the report.

The researchers argue that the importance of teachers in supporting and encouraging 'vulnerable' children and increasing their positive self-image whilst avoiding negative expectations and stereotypes has implications for recruiting the best teachers into schools in disadvantaged communities.

The implications of the study are:

⇨ Recruit the best teachers to schools in disadvantaged areas;

⇨ Assess children early and provide additional support classes and teaching where necessary;

⇨ Emphasise 'active cultivation' and 'parent power' in parenting classes and programmes;

⇨ Promote 'communities of learning' in the classroom so students can take responsibility for their and others' learning;

⇨ Schools and communities should provide extra educational experiences especially for 'vulnerable' children.

4 July 2011

Notes

1   Institute of Education, University of London

2   Birkbeck, University of London

3   University of Oxford

⇨ The above information is reprinted with kind permission from the Institute of Education, London. Visit www.ioe.ac.uk for more information.

© *Institute of Education, London*

INSTITUTE OF EDUCATION, LONDON

Why character skills are crucial in early years education

James Heckman's research into the benefits of concentrating on character over cognitive skills can help tackle inequality.

By Madeleine Bunting

A child in a welfare-dependent family hears on average 616 words an hour, according to a US study. It's twice that in a working-class home, and 2,153 words an hour in a professional home. In a typical hour, a child in a welfare-dependent family will hear five affirmations on average and 11 prohibitions, a child in a working-class home will hear 12 affirmations and seven prohibitions; a child in a professional home – 32 affirmations and five prohibitions.

Not only do children from better-off homes arrive at school with much better cognitive skills on average than from poorer homes, but they have also often benefited from the nurturing of 'soft skills'

This is the easiest way to sum up very quickly the scale and challenge of tackling inequality in developed countries, according to the American economics professor and Nobel Prize winner, and adviser to President Barack Obama, James Heckman. Not only do children from better-off homes arrive at school with much better cognitive skills on average than from poorer homes, but they have also often benefited from the nurturing of 'soft skills', which lay the crucial foundation for success in life – conscientiousness, persistence, openness to learning. It is these character skills that are far better predictors of all kinds of positive life outcomes.

What's more, Heckman warned, this kind of dramatic inequality produced by different parenting styles is becoming even more pronounced: educated working women are investing more time in their children (contrary to the kind of popular anxiety around working mothers) but poorly educated working women are investing less time in their children. 'In the next generation, a group of children will have had a major advantage and I would expect to see a big increase in inequality.'

Heckman believes there is a lot that the state can do to tackle inequality, and he laid them out in a lecture in London. The big mistake that governments in developed countries have made is to focus almost exclusively on education as the main way to tackle inequality. That has led to much too big an emphasis being placed on cognitive skills. In pursuit of higher standards, they have put in place a big apparatus to test and inspect schools, but many of these initiatives have had limited results. What they have missed is the far bigger issue of character. What secures good life outcomes is not cognitive skills but character skills. And many of them are formed in the family – so one of the most cost-effective interventions is in supporting or supplementing parenting. 'It sounds very dated and rather Victorian,' admitted Heckman.

The character skills that are crucial are summed up in Heckman's acronym 'Ocean': **o**penness (curiosity, willing to learn); **c**onsciousness (staying on task); **e**xtroversion (outgoing, friendly); **a**greeableness (helpful); **n**euroticism (attention to detail, persistence). These are the skills that enable children to learn; without them even the

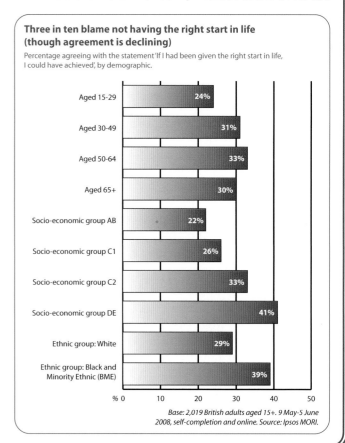

Three in ten blame not having the right start in life (though agreement is declining)

Percentage agreeing with the statement 'If I had been given the right start in life, I could have achieved', by demographic.

Aged 15-29	24%
Aged 30-49	31%
Aged 50-64	33%
Aged 65+	30%
Socio-economic group AB	22%
Socio-economic group C1	26%
Socio-economic group C2	33%
Socio-economic group DE	41%
Ethnic group: White	29%
Ethnic group: Black and Minority Ethnic (BME)	39%

% 0   10   20   30   40   50

Base: 2,019 British adults aged 15+. 9 May-5 June 2008, self-completion and online. Source: Ipsos MORI.

THE GUARDIAN

best teachers can do little. These are the skills that are predictive of outcomes such as educational achievement, obesity, offender rates, employment and smoking. The single biggest predictor of longevity and school achievement is conscientiousness – which is effectively a form of self-control.

> *While character was once thought immutable, there is now evidence that it is more malleable at two key points in the life cycle: the early years and then again in adolescence around 12-15*

One of the most important findings of the famous Perry preschool programme (for children from very low-income families), which Heckman has studied, was that it hugely improved children's life chances not because it had any impact on IQ (the initial improvement petered out) but because it helped children's character skills – such as self-control, regulating their own behaviour and reduced aggression. The Perry programme, which has been running for nearly 30 years, has been calculated to have made a seven to ten per cent rate of return given the huge savings in reduced criminal behaviour and welfare dependence.

The good news is that while character was once thought immutable, there is now evidence that it is more malleable at two key points in the life cycle: the early years and then again in adolescence around 12-15. Probably the most cost-effective policy tackling inequality would be interventions at these ages around

building character skills covered by Ocean. Precisely the kind of government programmes in early years and youth work that are being so badly hit in the cuts.

Heckman's argument is that inequality is inextricably linked with the challenge of improving productivity. Countries want to increase the latter to ensure a place in the global economy but they will not be able to do that unless their labour force has the skills and that is about reducing inequality. His concern is that there is a growing polarisation as more children than ever go to university at the same time as more children end up 'neets' – not in employment or education.

Here is a fascinating antidote to the kind of social mobility strategy announced by Nick Clegg recently, which ended up swamped in a wave of controversy about internships (and his experience of them). Where Clegg focused on measures of cognitive achievement – university entrance, for example – Heckman's suggestion is that the entire educational system needs to place much more emphasis on character building; this is what will prove more effective at raising standards but it will also provide the kind of employment skills needed. The majority of jobs are not intellectually complex, but they do require effective collaboration, confidence and motivation.

In many aspects, Heckman's research is an endorsement of the Labour investment in early years – though perhaps not of its policies pressing single parents into work – but the big challenge he presents to several decades of government policy is how character needs to be at the heart of education.

20 May 2011

© Guardian News and Media Limited 2011

An investment in the future...

THE GUARDIAN

Making the rich pay more is not social mobility

These Robin Hood plans over extra university places are a bit rich. Francesca Preece asks: Why are the wealthy paying for the failure of governments past and present to give the poor the same chance in education?

Just when you thought the furore over university fees had disappeared, it rears its ugly head again.

Minister David Willetts is under fire over proposals in his White Paper (out in the summer should you wish to obtain it for some light reading), where extra university places come at a hefty price. The idea is to allow over-subscribed universities the chance to get more students on their books by offering 'off-quota' places.

This new capacity is over and above existing student numbers and solely available to those who can pay – and pay a lot.

The places will be given on the understanding that students can: (a) cough up overseas students' prices (that will be £28k a year for medicine please) and (b) get the grades they were meant to get in the first place.

While the Government insists the rich can't just buy their way in, the scheme leaves a funny taste in this graduate's mouth.

Not because I don't think that it is wrong that a student with a bit more cash behind them can get a place thanks to their bank balance (I do), but because of the idea that this is social mobility in action.

Those seeking 'off-quota' places are still having to get the same grades as everyone else – it's not as if they're walking into Oxford with straight Ds. In the small print, students who take up these extra places won't be eligible for a state-funded loan. Coming up with £12k+ is not necessarily easy, even for those in the black.

It's the distinction and prejudice I don't like about all this. The Government is promoting a situation where the rich are treated differently from the rest of us. Wealth is excluding people from the education mainstream. Of course this may not harm them in an academic sense, but it will perpetuate the two-tiered system, between private and state schools, into higher education. EVERYONE should be entitled to the same high standard of education and the same opportunities. Equality should be for richer and for poorer.

I am not seeking to excuse the means by which money can be used to facilitate opportunities in education and work. I despised the Conservative auctioneering of an internship a few months back but I also despise the fact that education is a commodity that has to be bought and sold. It is a sad state of affairs that money is often the only answer in giving a child a better education.

In an ideal world there shouldn't be the need for a private education system. But why should the rich pay the price for the failures of governments past and present, to produce a state school system where children aren't ready for the world of work at 16? Whether we like it or not, it is not the fault of wealthy families that poorer students have failed to receive a good education. It is too easy to pin the blame on them or punish them for the mistakes of politicians.

Social mobility won't come from making the rich pay more. Why don't the universities justify their new prices by ploughing the money they are set to make from their £9k+ annual membership fees into scholarships? If the Government is so serious about social mobility, they will realise that it is education which is the key to unlocking a person's potential. With education and skills, a person can walk out into the world of work and self-dependency. Instead of bemoaning the circumstances of the rich why don't we try to afford the poor the same chances as them.

The hike in student fees wasn't exactly the answer to this. In a large number of jobs degrees are necessary to get your foot in the door. Yet despite this, the Coalition gave the green light to higher fees. Instead of giving more young adults a university education the Government's doing a great job of turning them away. Irrespective of whether rich kids pay more or not, it doesn't stop the simple fact that a huge number of students will steer clear of the higher education route because £27,000 in fees after three years is just not feasible. LEA help and student loans only go so far.

That is why I do back one plan in Willett's White Paper – getting businesses and charities to sponsor a student throughout his or her degree. Now that in my eyes is the real saving grace and argument for social mobility in action. It is the one way where everyone will be on the same playing field. The size of your brain will surpass the size of your wallet.

These academic apprenticeships should be applauded and I urge all businesses out there to put a £9,000 donation on a student's sponsoring form. It will be an investment for life.

11 May 2011

⇨ This article originally appeared on the Total Politics website www.totalpolitics.com/blog and is reprinted with their kind permission.

© Total Politics

Let's open up internships

Information from The Friend.

By Kayte Lawton

Internships can offer significant benefits to young people, but are out of reach for far too many.

Every year, thousands of young people desperately seek out the chance to work for free as unpaid interns in exciting and competitive industries like fashion, advertising, politics and the arts. The lucky ones will often find themselves working long hours doing jobs that many of their employers would admit are vital and would otherwise be done by paid staff.

It would be churlish to suggest that interns get nothing in return for their hard work. That is the whole point of an unpaid internship – people do them because the rewards are significant, including valuable experience, an address book full of contacts and sometimes a permanent role with the employer.

The problem is all those well-qualified, talented and passionate young people who lack the resources to pay their way through an unpaid internship. This means that the experiences and contacts that flow from an internship can be out of reach for young people from less well-off backgrounds.

Not only can it be hard to fund your way through an unpaid internship, but just hearing about these gold dust-like opportunities can be difficult without the right contacts. The Panel of Fair Access to the Professions, a body set up by Gordon Brown to look at how to get more young people from less-affluent families into professional jobs, found that internships could be vital. But worryingly, they concluded that internships often operate as part of an 'informal economy' where opportunities depend on personal contacts rather than proven ability or potential.

Much of journalism, politics, the arts and publishing is dominated by people from higher social classes who were privately educated or went to the top universities. We should reflect on the fact that many of the sectors in which unpaid internships are widespread wield considerable political or cultural power.

It is difficult to know how many people are working in unpaid internships at any one time because there is no agreed definition of what an internship is. However, a number of studies have given us an idea of the scale of the problem. The Chartered Institute of Personnel and Development found that a fifth of employers planned to hire at least one intern over the summer of 2010 and a survey by the training body Skillset found that nearly half the people working in the creative industries in 2008 had worked for free in the past.

In its recent annual report the Low Pay Commission, which monitors the minimum wage, says that there is 'systematic abuse of interns, with a growing number of people undertaking "work" but excluded from the minimum wage'. Unlike businesses, charities and other non-profit organisations including government bodies and community organisations are legally allowed to have unpaid interns doing proper work, because minimum wage legislation lets them take on 'voluntary workers'. Many charities take advantage of this, employing expenses-only interns in policy, research and campaigning roles; as does Parliament, which practically runs on the work of unpaid interns in both Houses – 'democracy on the cheap', as one campaigner puts it. There is no doubt that charities and government have limited resources available for covering the wages of interns. Yet many of these same organisations are rightly concerned about improving social mobility – relying so heavily on unpaid internships risks cutting across these objectives.

The key issue is to raise the number of paid internships offered. How could we encourage employers?

The Low Pay Commission has recommended that HM Revenue and Customs, which is responsible for enforcing minimum wage legislation, targets sectors that regularly advertise expenses-only internships. At the moment, the HMRC seems to be turning a blind eye to bad practice in the private sector.

Yet challenging the widespread use of unpaid internships does not rely simply on regulation and enforcement. Working with government, organisations which support businesses (like the CBI, the Federation of Small Businesses and sector-based employers' bodies) need to proactively provide guidance to employers about their legal obligations under minimum wage legislation.

Trade unions should seek out unpaid interns for 'test cases' to take to the employment tribunals to demonstrate to employers that illegal practices will not go unnoticed, something the National Union of Journalists is pursuing.

Large employers could work with smaller firms and charities to share interns, covering the full salary costs as part of their corporate social responsibility while working to broaden the skills and experience of their interns. An organisation called Charity Works currently offers graduate management-training programmes across six charities: this model could be expanded to include internships. The political blog Left Foot Forward recently launched a successful fundraising campaign to enable them to recruit their first paid intern.

Young people are already taking a hit from the recession and spending cuts, with high youth unemployment, the withdrawal of financial support for post-16 education, raising tuition fees and an unaffordable housing market. Let's not demand that they work for free too. Instead, let's help employers to create more paid opportunities and to open them up to a broader mix of people.

Kayte Lawton is the co-author of Why Interns Need a Fair Wage, *a joint report from the Institute for Public Policy Research and Internocracy. The report is available from www.ippr.org/publications*

10 February 2011

⇨ The above information is reprinted with kind permission from The Friend. Visit their website at http://thefriend.org for more information on this and other related topics.

© The Friend

Unpaid internships break the law – but only 10% know it

Research commissioned by Internocracy reveals that only 10% of under-35s who have heard of internships know their rights when it comes to working as an unpaid intern.

And employers aren't faring much better when it comes to understanding legislation around internships: only 12% of managers interviewed who have heard of internships, understand that for-profit companies may be breaking the law if they offer unpaid placements.

The results also found that 84% of employees who have worked in a company that employs interns think that they are a useful addition to their organisation.

It's clear that the business case of using unpaid interns is no more able to stand up to scrutiny than the legal or moral case.

Susan Nash, NUS Vice President (Society and Citizenship), says, 'With devastating levels of youth unemployment it is deeply concerning that so few employers and graduates are aware of the legislation around placements and internships. NUS is campaigning with other organisations and trade unions to see the legislation enforced and graduates protected from exploitative practices'.

Internocracy CEO Becky Heath said:

'When such low numbers of young people and employers actually understand the rights interns have in the workplace, it's no wonder that exploitation is rife in popular sectors where competition for experience is fierce.

'The reality is that if an organisation takes on someone to do work for them, whether or not they are called an "intern", they should be paid at least national minimum wage if they are being given responsibilities and are expected to work set hours. "Intern" isn't code for "free labour" and it's time companies stopped profiting from exploiting young people.'

Dom Potter, co-founder of Internocracy said:

'The last few weeks have seen the atrocious act of internships being auctioned off to the highest bidder at the Conservative annual ball. But in reality this is what happens every time an unpaid internship placement is filled: people with fewer financial means or social connections are priced out of the market. With youth unemployment at a record high and social mobility at an all-time low, we simply cannot afford for this broken system to continue.'

June 2011

⇨ The above information is reprinted with kind permission from the NUS. Visit www.nus.org.uk for more information.

© NUS

THE FRIEND / NUS

Decline in mid-wage jobs

'Shrinking middle' labour market trapping workers in low salary, low-skilled jobs, according to new report.

A rapid decline in mid-wage jobs is forcing many people to compete for low-wage work, risking waning social mobility as workers often get stuck on low salaries, according to a report published by The Work Foundation tomorrow (15 July). Mid-wage workers who were once employed in, for example, office administration or factory assembly roles, are being left with little option but to take on lower-waged, lower-skilled work as domestic cleaners, food service handlers or customer service advisors.

Tonight (14 July), Channel 4 News will air a special report on the research. They spoke to a number of people feeling the effects of this shift in the labour market including Phillip, who once worked in manufacturing. He is worried about the implications of taking an unskilled job and feels people will look at him and say, 'You have been pushing trolleys – why does that qualify you to do this skilled job?' In another interview, Will, a trained engineer who now works as a school janitor, said, 'I'm pretty much doing anything from cleaning toilets to moving.'

The Work Foundation research reveals that office administration and secretarial posts, which have traditionally been dominated by women, have been declining over the past ten years. This is in contrast to lower-waged 'caring service' occupations which are on the rise. Meanwhile, middle-waged roles such as plant processing and metal machinist jobs, which tend to be dominated by men, are disappearing due to technological advances.

The middle of the job market has been squeezed for over a decade, with strong growth in professional employment and in some lower-paying jobs. These changes have caused the labour market to become increasingly hourglass-shaped as the middle continues to hollow out.

Dr Paul Sissons, researcher at The Work Foundation and author of *The Hourglass and the Escalator: Labour market change and mobility*, said: 'In the recession and early recovery, high- and low-waged occupations have fared better. Those losing middle-skilled jobs and "bumping down" into lower-wage work can experience both a loss of income and an under-utilisation of skills. It is also the case that workers who move into low-wage work often find it difficult to move up the career ladder. While for those with the fewest skills, the increased competition for low-wage jobs means many struggle to find employment at all.

'Given that low-waged, low-skilled jobs are an enduring feature of the labour market, boosting the potential for in-work social mobility should be a priority for policymakers. The Government should focus on encouraging employers to develop career ladders for employees, and to support the long-term learning needs of workers so they can progress in their careers.'

Dr Neil Lee, senior economist at The Work Foundation, said: 'Politicians are very concerned about the squeezed middle and high costs erode mid-level incomes even further. But our research suggests they will increasingly need to consider the "shrinking middle", as mid-level jobs continue to disappear.'

This paper is the second in a series of publications from The Work Foundation's The Bottom Ten Million research programme, which focuses on the employment prospects of Britain's low earners between now and 2020. The programme seeks to identify the priority measures that need to be taken if they are not to be left behind.

Shaks Ghosh, chief executive of the Private Equity Foundation, which supports disadvantaged young people and is a sponsor of The Bottom Ten Million programme, said: 'With such a challenging employment outlook, understanding what jobs are available in the labour market is key to helping disadvantaged young people enter the world of work and reach their full potential. The issue of around one million young people not in education, employment or training needs urgent attention.'

Kenny Boyle, director of Working Links which also sponsors The Bottom Ten Million programme, said, 'Finding and keeping the right people is extremely important to a business, so it's important for providers of back-to-work programmes to work with businesses to not only help recruit employees but also train new and existing people to enable progression in the workplace. It's also vital that these organisations closely monitor trends and equip unemployed people with skills relevant to the local and regional labour markets.

'Our experience shows that, despite each industry and region being different, there are jobs out there. And given that under the Government's new Work Programme sustainability is key, we are actively working with employers to equip them with the right components to help grow their business, take on staff and progress their workforce.'

14 July 2011

⇨ The above information is reprinted with kind permission from The Work Foundation. Visit http://theworkfoundation.com for more.

© The Work Foundation

THE WORK FOUNDATION

⇨ The latest DWP press release says benefit fraud is now £1.6bn: 0.7% of the benefits bill. Meanwhile, £15bn was officially caught in tax fraud, while estimated tax avoidance is £70bn. (page 6)

⇨ A poll for *The Times* in 2009 found that 57 per cent of people are in favour of keeping the higher tax rate, while just 22 per cent oppose it. (page 7)

⇨ This study of inherited wealth from 1984 to 2005 found that rising house prices pushed up the value of inheritances from being worth 3% of GDP in 1984 to about 4.3% in 2005 and there is a 'high degree of inequality' in the distribution of inheritances. (page 8)

⇨ A new report from BritainThinks shows a huge rise in the country's aspirations, with seven in ten Britons now viewing themselves as middle class, compared with a quarter a generation ago. (page 9)

⇨ The average working-class household income is £24,000. (page 9)

⇨ The most important factor defining a person's class is 'level of education', according to 23 per cent of people surveyed, followed by 'their parents' class' (21 per cent), 'the nature of their job' (20 per cent) and 'their income' (20 per cent). (page 10)

⇨ There has always been an association between health and social class and, despite the welfare state and the improvement in health in all sections of societies over the years, this discrepancy remains. (page 11)

⇨ The Marmot Review identified that people living in the poorest areas die on average seven years earlier than people living in richer areas and spend up to 17 more years living with poor health. (page 13)

⇨ Researchers at the University of California found that it takes longer for a family's economic and social status to change since the Industrial Revolution than it did during earlier periods of human history. (page 14)

⇨ More people think they have been upwardly mobile (that they have a job that is 'higher' up the occupational scale than their father's) than think they have moved downwards. (page 15)

⇨ Almost one in five children receive free school meals, yet this group accounts for fewer than one in a hundred Oxbridge students. (page 17)

⇨ The UK has one of the lowest rates of social mobility in the developed world. (page 21)

⇨ Irrespective of family income levels, students who receive excellent A-Levels have roughly the same rate of entry to Oxbridge. The problem is that students from relatively poor families are far less likely to get those A-Levels than those from relatively well-off families. Students on free school meals perform disproportionately badly across the board in A-Level results. (page 23)

⇨ Only around three-quarters of children from the poorest fifth of families reach the expected Key Stage 2 level at age 11, compared with 97 per cent of children from the richest fifth. (page 25)

⇨ Only 37 per cent of the poorest mothers said they hoped their child would go to university, compared with 81 per cent of the richest mothers. (page 26)

⇨ Only 21 per cent of the poorest fifth (measured by parental socioeconomic position) manage to gain five good GCSEs, compared to 75 per cent of the top quintile – a gap of 54 percentage points. (page 27)

⇨ Poverty has a much greater influence on how White British pupils do at school than it does on the academic performance of other ethnic groups, two new studies have concluded. (page 29)

⇨ A comprehensive-school student with A-Level grades BBB is likely to perform as well in their university degree as an independent- or grammar-school student with A-Level grades ABB or AAB – i.e. one to two grades higher. (page 32)

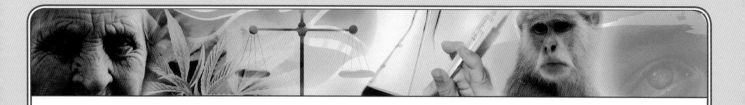

Blue-collar worker

This refers to someone who is in a traditionally working-class job – that is, manual labourers (based on the idea that historically, manual and industrial workers would wear overalls to work which were often blue).

'Chav'

A derogatory slang word, 'chav' characterises a stereotype of a working-class person who dresses and behaves in a certain way. Elements of this stereotype may include Burberry fashion wear, tracksuits, 'hoodies', baseball caps and chunky jewellery, as well as associations with binge drinking, claiming benefits, petty crime and yobbism. Some see the ridicule of the 'chav' and its application to underprivileged young people as an excuse for persecution of the working classes.

Elitism

If something is referred to as elitist, this means it favours the privileged few rather than being based on fairness and equality.

FSM

This stands for Free School Meals. In reports and studies dealing with the subject of social mobility, a child's 'FSM status' (whether or not they are in receipt of free school meals) is often used as a measure of their social background and level of wealth.

Meritocracy

A system of government whereby positions are gained not through social class or wealth but through individual merit and ability.

Middle England/Middle Britain

Middle England (or sometimes, Middle Britain) is increasingly used as a socio-economic reference point instead of middle class. It encompasses a wider range of characteristics than simply income, career and education, although there is no single definition. It can be seen as overlapping with other social groups identified by politicians, such as Ed Miliband's 'squeezed middle' and Nick Clegg's 'Alarm Clock Britons'.

Social class

Class refers to a hierarchy which exists among social groups in the UK. Traditionally, people belonged to one of three classes – working, middle and upper – based on the status ascribed to them by their occupation and economic position. Massive social and economic shifts in the 20th century led to what many felt was the death of social class, but most would argue that a class system still exists in a different form and is a major part of the collective British consciousness today. It has become a very complex (not to say contentious) issue to define one's social class, factoring in such issues as background and upbringing, accent, manners, culture, education, career and postcode as well as wealth.

Social engineering

Attempting to fix social problems and manufacture a social system to a pre-decided pattern.

Social mobility

The ability of an individual to move around within the class system. In the past, social mobility was an almost unheard-of concept, whereas today we would think little of the daughter of a builder growing up to become an accountant, or a doctor's son forgoing higher education and training as a plumber. However, there are worries that the progress of social mobility in the UK is slowing.

'Underclass'

This is a term which is being used increasingly often in the press to describe a group who they feel ought not to be described as working class, since they do not work. It refers to those who exist within what is often called the 'dependency culture': a social group who do not earn but instead subsist on state benefits. Like 'chav', the term has been accused of creating a negative stereotype of working-class people and demonising those who require state welfare.

White-collar worker

This refers to someone who is in a traditionally middle-class career – a professional, or clerical worker (based on the idea that historically, male office workers would wear a white dress shirt to work).

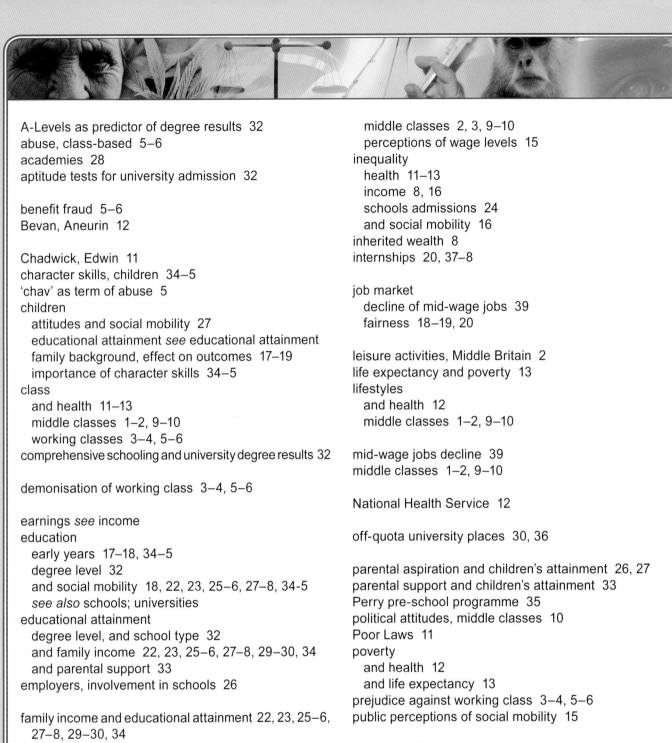

ACKNOWLEDGEMENTS

The publisher is grateful for permission to reproduce the following material.

While every care has been taken to trace and acknowledge copyright, the publisher tenders its apology for any accidental infringement or where copyright has proved untraceable. The publisher would be pleased to come to a suitable arrangement in any such case with the rightful owner.

Chapter One: Class and Inequality

Uncovered: the real Middle Britain, © Experian, *Celebrate your identity! That is, know your place,* © Spiked Online, *Chav: the vile word at the heart of fractured Britain,* © Guardian News and Media Limited 2011, *The 50p tax rate must go – but scrapping it could provoke an all-out class war,* © Telegraph Media Group Limited 2011, *Inherited wealth and inequality,* © ToUChstone blog, *Seven in ten of us belong to Middle Britain,* © The Independent, *Health and social class,* © Patient UK.

Chapter Two: Social Mobility

Social mobility 'slower than in medieval England', © politics.co.uk, *How fair is the route to the top?,* © NatCen, *Pitfalls on the path to social mobility,* © Institute for Fiscal Studies, *Opening doors, breaking barriers,* © Crown copyright is reproduced with the permission of Her Majesty's Stationery Office, *Clegg targets unpaid internships,* © Guardian News and Media Limited 2011, *Tackling inequality is key to improving social mobility, Mr Clegg,* © One Society, *Upwardly mobile?,* © Economic and Social Research Council, *Schools and social mobility,* © Adam Smith Institute, *Class divides our schools,* © Guardian News and Media Limited 2010, *The gap years: education and social immobility,* © Economic and Social Research Council, *Involving employers in schools can encourage social mobility,* © Children & Young People Now, *Children's education crucial for social mobility,* © Economic and Social Research Council, *Academies will struggle to break public schools' grip on top jobs,* © Total Politics, *Class has much bigger effect on white pupils' results,* © British Educational Research Association, *Education isn't a zero-sum game,* © Adam Smith Institute, *Social mobility: a case for grammar schools?,* © Political Reboot, *Higher education outcomes,* © Sutton Trust, *How do disadvantaged children succeed against the odds?,* © Institute of Education, London, *Why character skills are crucial in early years education,* © Guardian News and Media Limited 2011, *Making the rich pay more is not social mobility,* © Total Politics, *Let's open up internships,* © The Friend, *Unpaid internships break the law – but only 10% know it,* © NUS, *Decline in mid-wage jobs,* © The Work Foundation.

Illustrations

Pages 4, 11, 21, 24: Don Hatcher; pages 6, 14, 23, 37: Simon Kneebone; pages 7, 20, 29, 35: Angelo Madrid; pages 9, 15: Bev Aisbett.

Cover photography

Left: © Jenny Rollo. Centre: © Patrick Leahy. Right: © Vailiki.

Additional acknowledgements

With thanks to the Independence team: Mary Chapman, Sandra Dennis and Jan Sunderland.

Lisa Firth
Cambridge
January, 2012

ASSIGNMENTS

The following tasks aim to help you think through the debate surrounding social mobility and provide a better understanding of the topic.

1 Watch an episode of the ITV period drama 'Downton Abbey'. How have society's attitudes to social class evolved since the period in which the drama was set? Are there any ways in which the class distinctions shown in the programme have not changed?

2 What would you say defines a person's class? Is it only about income, or are there other factors involved? Do you think people still tend to identify themselves as belonging to a particular class in today's society?

3 'This house believes that words like "chav" are used to unfairly demonise the working class and perpetuate a stereotype of a feckless underclass.' Debate this motion as a class, with one half arguing in favour and the other against.

4 Read two different newspapers for a fortnight. Choose newspapers which have different political stances: for example, the 'Daily Mail' and the 'Guardian', or the 'Telegraph' and the 'Independent'. Cut out any stories which reference class. At the end of two weeks, review the stories you have collected. What conclusions can you draw about the way the newspapers view different classes? How do you think this influences their readers?

5 Read the book 'Chavs' by Owen Jones and write a review. Do you agree or disagree with the arguments put forward by the writer?

6 'There is no such thing as class these days: the "upstairs, downstairs" culture of yesteryear has long since passed away. Those who claim their class has held them back are just making excuses.' Do you think there is any truth in this view? Discuss your views in small groups.

7 Carry out a survey asking people to rank the following in order of how damaging they feel each one is to the country and economy: benefit fraud, large corporate bonuses, tax evasion, dependency culture. Analyse your results: what conclusions can you draw?

8 Find out more about Aneurin 'Nye' Bevan, the Labour politician often credited as the architect of the National Health Service. Write a short biography covering his life, views and achievements.

9 Many people, including Sir Peter Lampl of the Sutton Trust, believe that increasing the number of grammar schools will improve social mobility in this country. Do you think there is a case for more grammar schools? What benefits and flaws does the grammar school system entail? Write an essay summarising the case for and against and drawing your own conclusions.

10 Find out more about the Government's 'Pupil Premium' policy. Do you think this will increase social mobility?

11 'Why should the rich be taxed more to help provide for the poor? They have worked hard for their money and the state has no right to deprive them of it. Ultimately, high taxes will result in them leaving the country and the economy will suffer.' Do you agree with this argument? Write an article summarising your views.

12 Find out about Nick Clegg's plans to make internships fairer. What criticisms were levelled at the Deputy Prime Minister following his announcement?

13 The 50p tax rate has been hotly debated recently: the article on page 7 is just one of the opinions put forward as part of this debate. Find out more about the 50p tax rate. Do you think it should be kept or scrapped? Write a short article explaining what the 50p tax rate is, why it is significant and the arguments in favour of keeping or scrapping it, summarised in simple terms.

14 Write three diary entries, covering a typical day in the life of a working-class person in 1911, 1951 and 2011. What employment would they be likely to have? What would their prospects be? How would their daily lives differ, and in what ways would there be similarities?

15 'Our MPs are the last people who should decide policies on social mobility, given their own privileged backgrounds.' Is this a fair statement? Discuss your views in pairs.